GAMES TRAINERS PLAY
Experiential Learning Exercises

GAMES TRAINERS PLAY
Experiential Learning Exercises

John W. Newstrom

University of Minnesota

AND

Edward E. Scannell

Arizona State University

McGraw-Hill, Inc.
New York St. Louis San Francisco Auckland Bogotá
Caracas Lisbon London Madrid Mexico City Milan
Montreal New Delhi San Juan Singapore
Sydney Tokyo Toronto

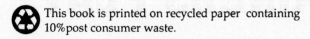
Library of Congress Cataloging in Publication Data

Newstrom, John W.
    Games trainers play.

    1. Small groups. 2. Group relations training.
3. Games. I. Scannell, Edward E., joint author. II.
Title.
HM133.N49   302.3'4   80-10870
ISBN 0-07-046408-1

GAMES TRAINERS PLAY: Experiential Learning Exercises

26 27 28 29 MALMAL 9 8 7 6 5

The editor was James J. Walsh, the production supervisors
were Marie Birdsall and Annette Bodzin, and the designer
was Jane Moorman.

Malloy Lithographing Inc. was the printer and binder.

This book is dedicated
to those special people
in our lives who have
helped us become better
trainers.

Table of Contents

Publisher's Note

Games Trainers Play (which was originally published in 1980) is the first of three books in a highly successful series compiled by John W. Newstrom and Edward E. Scannell. The success of Games Trainers Play stimulated the development of a second book of entirely different "games," which was published in 1983 under the title More Games Trainers Play. As a result of popular demand, the authors have created (with input from many experienced trainers) a third book in the series, Still More Games Trainers Play (published in 1991).

Users of the other two books have found them to be invaluable aids in a wide variety of training situations. The books have received high praise from reviewers and should be on every trainer's bookshelf.

Preface

When Games Trainers Play was first published in 1980, we could not anticipate the very positive response from tens of thousands of trainers around the globe. That enthusiasm from our HRD colleagues encouraged us to develop a sequel, More Games Trainers Play, which was published in 1983.

It seems that the entire field of experiential learning continues to enjoy an enthusiastic reception. On that basis we have developed a third book in this series, Still More Games Trainers Play.

We're often asked, "How did this all start?" Having conducted numerous "Train the Trainer" workshops for the American Society of Training and Development, we became very much aware of the need for activities and exercises to supplement the instructional phase of the program. Collecting the dozens of "games" was an enjoyable experience. All of these exercises have been field-tested and are presented to our readers with the conviction that they deliver as promised.

The format for each game follows this outline:

TITLE
OBJECTIVE
PROCEDURE
DISCUSSION QUESTIONS
MATERIALS REQUIRED
APPROXIMATE TIME REQUIRED
SOURCE

Whenever possible, we have identified the primary source or contributor of the activity. Since many games are generic, it has not always been possible to locate the original source. While we appreciate the numerous friends and associates who have sent us items, we apologize if we have failed to acknowledge an earlier source.

A sincere and warm acknowledgment is given to Betty Norris and her co-worker Rachelle Maxwell for their dedication and expertise in taking scribbled notes and scratched-over manuscripts and transforming them into a handsome piece of work.

John W. Newstrom, Duluth, Minnesota
Edward E. Scannell, Tempe, Arizona

The authors gratefully acknowledge the typing assistance of
Mrs. Robert Norris, Mrs. James Blake, and Mrs. John Newstrom.

John W. Newstrom
Edward E. Scannell

Introduction

Definition of Games

Professional trainers are responsible for managing the content, process, and environment of a learning situation. Content refers to the facts, data, information, and rules deemed important to ultimate application on the job. Process encompasses the approaches by which that content is delivered. Environment is the physical and psychological surroundings for the training session (location, facilities, arrangements, food, etc.).

This book focuses on games professional trainers and educators can, and do, play. These games are part of the process element of a learning experience. In this book, a game may be an exercise, illustration, activity, or incident used to present or support the trainee's learning. The uniqueness of the game itself will often be sufficient to draw additional attention to the point made, and thereby reinforce it.

Learning, of course, can take place at three levels--cognitive, affective, or psychomotor. The acquisition of knowledge, attitudes, or skills can be expedited through the selective utilization of an appropriate game.

Games vs. Other Experiential Exercises

Games, as used here, differ from most other experiential exercises, such as simulations, board games, computer exercises, role plays, or in-basket exercises. Although it is difficult to generalize, simulations usually attempt to create some significant aspect of a complex organization, and provide an opportunity for realistic implementation of a solution. A range of interrelated factors are often present at both micro and macro levels, and there is often a longitudinal time dimension built into the process. As such, experiential exercises and simulations often require a greater time commitment and are more complex in their set-up, operation, and interpretation.

An explanation of the typical characteristics of games will show the marked contrast involved. The point is that games are not advocated here as either better than other approaches or as a replacement for them. Games are different, and will be seen as having unique features making them appropriate for other objectives.

Characteristics of Games

Games usually:

1. Are brief. They can range from a one-minute visual illus-

tration or verbal vignette up to a 30-minute group discussion exercise. However, since they are used for supplementing other material, the time devoted to them should be minimized.

2. Are inexpensive. In general, nothing has to be purchased commercially; nor does a consultant need to be engaged. With rare exceptions, the games included here can be used at no cost.

3. Are participative. To be effective, games must involve the trainees physically(through movement) or psychologically (through visual and mental attention). Games draw the trainees' attention, and make them think, react, or laugh.

4. Use props. Several of the games involve the use of a simple prop to add realism to the activity. The prop may be a picture, bag of lemons, sport coat, or deck of cards.

5. Are low-risk. All of the games presented here have been tested many times. If matched to the right context, and applied in a positive and professional manner, they will almost always succeed.

6. Are adaptable. The best games, like the best humorous stories, can be adapted to fit any situation and reinforce several different points. They can often be modified slightly and still retain their original flavor and character.

7. Are single-focus. In contrast to simulations, games are often used to illustrate a single point only. As such, they are oriented to micro issues rather than interdependent macro issues.

Proper Uses of Games

An examination of the more than 100 games in this book will reveal that each has a distinctive purpose. They can, however, be classified in various ways according to their general applications. The major objectives are:

1. As session icebreakers. Good trainers catch and hold the group's attention at the beginning of each session. Games are useful devices to "warm up" a group, and a pattern of games used like this creates further expectations in the minds of the trainees.

2. To involve the trainees. Many games require a verbal response, physical movement, or intellectual activity. Consequently, they invoke the use of participation in a positive manner.

3. As illustrations. Extensive presentation of concepts, theories, and models will bore almost any audience. Games can provide vivid examples that will be implanted in trainee memories for longer periods of time. In short, a change of pace may be just what the doctor ordered.

4. As session closings. In addition to summarizing, professional trainers incorporate some device to add "zing" to the end of a long hour or day. Further, they attempt to stimulate the trainees to action. Several of the games are designed to facilitate transfer of learning from the training context to the work environment.

Improper Uses of Games

There are many pitfalls in the use of games as a training tool. Insecure, inexperienced, or unprepared trainers may use games to kill time, to impress upon trainees how smart they are, or to put down trainees. When playing the games begins to dominate the focus of the learning process, most trainees will perceive the games as being hokey or cute, but distracting from the overall professionalism of the program. Trainees should be encouraged to ask the questions of "so what?" or "what's in it for me?" from each game and should always find at least one answer. Finally, good games should be neither overly complicated, nor should they in any way be personally threatening or demeaning to the participant.

Facilitation of Learning

Several classical principles of learning are incorporated into the use of games. A few of these will be briefly highlighted here.

1. Repetition: retention of new material or a new skill will be increased if the trainee hears it more than once or practices a new behavior several times. Insertion of a game into a training module allows the trainer to reiterate a point in another fashion and thereby increase the probability of retention and application.

2. Reinforcement: many of the games described in this book provide an opportunity for success or achievement on the part of the participants. By providing pleasant consequences for their behavior, that behavior is reinforced and consequently is more likely to be repeated in the future.

3. Association: much of our learning is not totally new, but is tangential to what is already known. In other words, it is often easier for us to move gradually from a base of knowledge to the unknown. Games--even familiar ones--help us to make the kind of connections between different contexts that ease the process of learning. Later on, the trainee may first recall the game, but then can make an easy transition to the underlying principle.

4. Senses: researchers tell us that learning is more effective when increasing numbers of the five basic senses are involved (sight, sound, speech, smell, and touch). Games generally build upon all but smell, and thereby add a second or third dimension to the classical learning process.

New and Different Games

The games contained in this book represent only a small sample of those popularly used in education and training today. Readers are encouraged to screen these games, pilot-test them to determine their own comfort level, and then use selected games to provide a refreshing change of pace to their programs. A second suggestion is to become an astute observer of other trainers and speakers, thereby acquiring an expanded set of trainer's games. A third recommendation is to develop your own set of games. This process should begin with clear answers to the questions of "What are my goals? How much time do I have? Who will be participating? What point am I trying to illustrate? How will my trainees respond?"

Conclusion

Training is a very serious business. Looked upon as the core of a training program, trainer's games are doomed to mockery and failure. When viewed as useful supplements to be used occasionally to reinforce and strengthen learning, games assume their rightful position in a subordinate role. Trainers who are willing to experiment with some new tools to enhance personal effectiveness should benefit greatly from these games.

I
CONFERENCE LEADERSHIP

The Advance Letter

Objective:

To relate trainee needs to program objectives.

Procedure:

Approximately two to four weeks before the beginning of a supervisory/management development seminar, letters are sent to each trainee's immediate supervisor asking the supervisor to respond to the single question, "What is this person's most important developmental need?"

As a second step, trainees are asked to respond in writing during the first hour of the actual program (or the warmup session on the previous evening) to the following questions: (1) "What is your most important developmental need?" and (2) "What does your boss think is your most important developmental need?"

Alternatives:

    1. The feedback can be provided to the trainees on an individual basis, rather than collectively. This procedure serves to heighten the impact of the process.
    2. The trainees and their bosses can be asked to conduct the process in advance, including face-to-face discussions of their perceptions. This has the advantage of high probability learner readiness. The inherent disadvantage is the possibility that not all supervisor-subordinate pairs will seriously complete the process in advance.
    3. Based on the collective feedback, the time allocated to various seminar topics can be shifted to better match the group's needs.

Discussion Questions:

    1. How similar/different are your perceptions of your needs from the perceptions of your supervisor?
    2. Why did some members' perceptions differ from their bosses' perceptions?
    3. Why did some members' perceptions of their needs differ from their thoughts about their bosses' perceptions?

Materials Required:

A standard letter for bosses, a standard form for trainees to complete, and flipcharts to post the results.

<u>Approximate Time Required:</u>

About 10 minutes for trainees to complete their forms; 10 to 20
minutes for discussion-oriented collection of perceptions and post-
ing of group results.

<u>Source:</u>

Attributed to Ken Hall and Ray Higgins of Armour-Dial.

Roles of a Trainer

Objective:

To reach an understanding (contract) between trainer and trainee about the trainer's intended role in the session.

Procedure:

At the beginning of a session, invite the trainees to express to the group the various roles, attitudes, and behaviors they expect (or wish) the trainer to play or portray for them. List these on a chalkboard or flipchart. Then share with them a previously-prepared set of your intended roles for that session (an example of some of the characteristics of a facilitative mode is shown on the following page). Then proceed to reconcile the two lists.

Discussion Questions:

1. What do you expect in the session that I do not intend to provide? What is the source of your expectations (e.g., prior educational experiences, wishful thinking)?
2. What do I intend to provide that you did not expect?
3. Do you anticipate any problems reconciling your expectations with my objections? If so, what can I/you do to prevent such problems?

Materials Required:

Handout or transparency with list of intended roles.

Approximate Time Required:

5-15 minutes

Source:

Unknown

Example
Roles of a Trainer (Facilitator)

1. Challenges thinking

2. Creates lists

3. Summarizes

4. Shares ideas

5. Provides handouts

6. Serves as a model

7. Raises questions

8. Guides discussion

9. Restates ideas

10. Provides constructive criticism

7

Thought Page

Objective:

To sensitize trainees to the need of focusing 100% of their energies on the seminar, excluding all other work-related and personal concerns.

Procedure:

Prepare a handout with directions similar to those on the following page. Distribute it to the participants early in the seminar, preferably within the first 15 minutes of introductory materials. Provide adequate time for the group to "dump" their thoughts and feelings onto the paper. Distribute envelopes to each person so they may enclose the form, seal the envelope, and attach their name to it. Then collect the envelopes as further symbolic evidence of the participants "disowning" their problems for the duration of the program. Finally, distribute the envelopes back to the participants during the closing moments of the program. (At this point, you may wish to ask if anyone wants to "trade" problems with someone else, or if they wish for you to "keep" their problems.)

1. A sample statement follows this page.
2. Examples of previous "thoughts" include:

    a. Prepare the budget for next year.
    b. Buy an anniversary present for my spouse.
    c. Call the airlines for vacation reservations.
    d. What to do with project XYZ.
    e. Visit Aunt Sue while here in town.

Alternatives:

In small groups, and where a considerable level of trust is already established (or, as a vehicle for establishing trust), you might handle the procedure orally. Then the leader as well as the participants can be more aware of the infusion of these thoughts into later discussions.

Materials Required:

One handout and one envelope for each participant.

Time Required:

10 minutes

Source: Unknown

Thought Page

<u>Introduction</u>:

Many of us come to a seminar, workshop, meeting, or retreat with a lot of things on our minds: a subordinate has not been producing as you expected, your boss recently made an unfavorable policy decision, your secretary is pregnant, the budget is due next week, etc. For the most part, (1) you cannot <u>solve</u> those problems while you are here, and (2) thinking about them during the seminar will <u>detract</u> from your involvement and potential learning.

<u>Directions</u>:

In the next 5 minutes, briefly list the major non-seminar thoughts running through your mind. These might relate to work, family, money, religion, politics, or your social life. Then seal this page in the envelope provided, placing your name on the front. (The envelope will be returned to you at the end of the seminar.) Now, <u>forget</u> about these problems!

(1)

(2)

(3)

(4)

(5)

(6)

(7)

(8)

(9)

(10)

Graffiti Feedback Boards

Objective:

To provide an anonymous outlet for ongoing trainee reactions.

Procedure:

Most reaction-based evaluation systems gather data at the end of a session or program, or possibly at a future date (a notable exception is the Instant Evaluation Form exercise in this book). The motivation to treat these seriously is lessened by the fact that changes will occur too late to improve the quality of the current session.

An informal alternative is the use of graffiti boards. Through the use of poster boards, flipcharts, or chalkboards, participants may express (ventilate) a variety of observations, reactions, ideas, or emotions to the trainer or the group. This may be done on a relatively anonymous basis. Topics may be provided at the top (e.g., "course content," "physical facilities," etc.) or the feedback may be solicited on a totally unstructured basis. In any case, an important outlet for emotional and intellectual catharsis has been provided.

Discussion Questions:

1. How many of you agree with the comment made about _____?
2. What is the basis for the various comments?
3. What corrective steps can we take now to change the situation?

Materials Required:

Flipchart or similar medium on which to write.

Approximate Time Required:

None for collecting the comments; varied amount of time for discussion.

Source:

Emily Hitchins, "Graffiti Provides Useful Feedback," Training, August, 1979, p. 12.

Group Movement

Objectives:

    1. To add the dimension of motion to training classes.
    2. To create opportunities for additional inter-participant interaction.

Procedure:

Most trainees in extended seminars will identify a favorite seat or area and cling closely to it for the duration of the program. Resolve to break up these familiar seating patterns for the benefit of the participants. This can be achieved by:

    1. Switching session set-ups from classroom to auditorium to round-table formats and letting members locate new seats.
    2. Switching the sizes of work groups for various small-group discussions (e.g., from three persons to six persons).
    3. Sorting trainees into different physical locations according to their views when they disagree on a topic. As reports are presented from the subgroups, allow converts to physically relocate to the other side.
    4. Asking participants to select the person whom they (a) know the least about, (b) identify most closely with, or (c) feel most in disagreement with, and seek out that person as their conversational partner for the next several minutes.

Materials Required:

None

Approximate Time Required:

5 minutes per move

Source:

Adapted from Judith H. Steele, "Five Ways to Get Trainees to Open Up and Get Moving," Training, November, 1978, pp. 40-42.

The Art of Seeking Good Questions

Objective:

To stimulate reflection and active response from participants through the phrasing/timing of questions.

Procedure:

Most good seminar leaders want active participation from trainees at some points in the program. Most participants have some relevant experiences to share and they want to participate in the discussion. Other persons may have legitimate questions because of confusion over an issue. How, then, can a trainer stimulate active participation? The answer may lie in these suggestions:

1. Lay out your expectation for questions early in the program. Inform the participants that you encourage and expect questions. (It's OK to ask questions.)
2. Respond positively to the first question asked. Trainees will be observing you closely to determine how serious you were.
3. Watch non-verbal behavior. You can often detect a desire to ask a question or challenge a point from facial expressions/body posture without waiting for someone to interject or raise their hand.
4. Remind the group that there are no stupid questions, just stupid answers. (See the "Dumb Joke" exercise.)
5. Repeat (or rephrase) the question to clarify your understanding of it, and to ensure that all other trainees heard it.
6. Pause after calling for questions. Five or ten seconds may seem like a long time, but the pressure is equally high on the group.
7. Never ask if there are any questions immediately before scheduled coffee breaks, meal time, or dismissal time. The higher priority of these events will either inhibit questioning or make the questioner very unpopular.
8. Specifically include several brief question and answer periods in your printed agenda or schedule. This alerts trainees to anticipate a call for questions.
9. Don't imply that you are rushed for time, but (reluctantly) could answer one or two questions. It will be very clear that you prefer none.

Materials Required:

None, except changes in your agenda.

Approximate Time Required:

Virtually none

Source:

Adapted from Milt Badt, "Ways to Encourage Your Trainees to Ask Questions," Training, May, 1978, pp. 74-5.

18

Instructional Objectives

Objective:

To vividly illustrate the key characteristics of training objectives.

Procedure:

Present a brief lecturette on the elements of effective training objectives (e.g., Bob Mager includes the activity to be performed, the resources to be provided, the constraints placed upon the trainee, and the standards of performance to be applied, such as quantity, quality, and speed.) Illustrations of imprecise and more precise (action) verbs to describe behaviors can be provided.

As the second stage (demonstration) in the training process, distribute the form found on the following page to the group, describing it as an exercise in the application of the previously-discussed principles. Keep a straight face until they have had a chance to read a few of the items and discover its true purpose. They will not only appreciate the intended humor involved, but also knowingly relate many of their own educational experiences where they were assigned "comparable" examination questions. After the laughter has died away, proceed to accent the ways in which many of the test questions actually apply Mager's principles.

Discussion Questions:

　　1. Have you ever encountered examination questions like these in the past? If so, what were your feelings at the time (frustration, hopelessness, etc.)?
　　2. What characteristics of good instructional objectives do you see in examples (action verbs, resources, constraints, performance criteria)?
　　3. What lessons are there here for the construction of instructional objectives (e.g., make sure they can be achieved within the training environment)?

Materials Required:

Copies of the following page.

Approximate Time Required:

5-10 minutes (following the lecturette, and preceding any follow-up practice sessions)

Source: Various, including Paul Dean in the Arizona Republic.

Examples of Instructional Objectives

Instructions: Read each question carefully. Answer all questions. Time limit: 4 hours. Begin immediately.

History: Describe the history of the papacy from its origins to the present day, concentrating especially, but not exclusively, on its social, political, economic, religious, and philosophical impact on Europe, Asia, America, and Africa. Be brief, concise, and specific.

Medicine: You have been provided with a razor blade, a piece of gauze, and a bottle of scotch. Remove your appendix. Do not suture until your work has been inspected. You have 15 minutes.

Public Speaking: 2,500 riot-crazed aborigines are storming the classroom. Calm them. You may use any ancient language except Latin or Greek.

Biology: Create Life. Estimate the differences in subsequent human culture if this form of life had developed 500 million years earlier, with special attention to its probable effect on the English parliamentary system. Prove your thesis.

Music: Write a piano concerto. Orchestrate and perform it with flute and drum. You will find a piano under your seat.

Psychology: Based on your knowledge of their works, evaluate the emotional stability, degree of adjustment and repressed frustrations of each of the following: Alexander of Aphrodisias, Rameses II, Gregory of Nicia, Hammurabi. Support your evaluation with quotations from each man's work, making appropriate references. It is not necessary to translate.

Sociology: Estimate the sociological problems which might accompany the end of the world. Construct an experiment to test your theory.

Engineering: The disassembled parts of a high-powered rifle have been placed on your desk. You will also find an instructional manual, printed in Swahili. In 10 minutes, a hungry Bengal tiger will be admitted to the room. Take whatever action you feel appropriate. Be prepared to justify your decision.

Economics: Develop a realistic plan for refinancing the national debt. Trace the possible effects of your plan in the following areas: Cubism, the Donatist controversy, the wave theory of light. Outline a method for preventing these effects. Point out the deficiencies in your point of view, as demonstrated in your answer to the last question.

21

<u>Political Science</u>: There is a red telephone on the desk beside you.
Start World War III. Report at length on its socio-political effects
if any.

<u>Epistemology</u>: Take a position for or against truth. Prove the
validity of your stand.

<u>Physics</u>: Explain the nature of matter. Include in your answer an
evaluation of the impact of the development of mathematics on
science.

<u>Philosophy</u>: Sketch the development of human thought; estimate its
significance. Compare with the development of any other kind of
thought.

<u>General Knowledge</u>: Describe in detail. Be objective and specific.

Swap Shop

<u>Objective</u>:

To cultivate a number of new ideas and to encourage group participation.

<u>Procedure</u>:

Everyone is told <u>in advance</u> to bring at least one idea, exercise, activity, etc., to the next training session. These should be focused around some central theme (e.g., how to handle "problem" trainees).

As each person describes his or her idea to the group, a panel of "experts" (three selected class members) instantly "rate" the idea on prepared flash cards (1-10, with 10 being high). The facilitator tabulates each total and announces the winners at the end of the time period.

<u>Discussion Questions</u>:

    1. How many people gained at least one useful new idea today?
    2. Did this process spark any additional ideas in your mind?
    3. Can you think of some other areas in which this method can be applied?
    4. What are some other variations on this technique?

<u>Materials Required</u>:

Three sets of flash cards (5 x 8 index cards), each set with a number from 1-10.

<u>Approximate Time Required</u>:

20-25 minutes

<u>Source</u>:

Unknown

Goal Setting / Action Planning

<u>Objective</u>:

To establish a positive climate and spirit of cooperation among persons who will be working together on future projects; to introduce teamwork into group activity.

<u>Procedure</u>:

Divide the group into teams of 4-6 each. (Grouping may be done along departmental lines, or strictly on a random, convenience basis.) Ask the group to spend the first 10 minutes developing a collective mental image (verbalized) of what their work situation would preferably be like a year from now (e.g., "What could it potentially become from a positive viewpoint?") Then ask each group to develop a skeletal action plan listing the items directly or indirectly under their control that must be accomplished in the next year to achieve the overall image. Now have each team present a brief report to the total group.

<u>Discussion Questions</u>:

1. How feasible is your overall plan? Will you have achieved your desired objectives a year from now?
2. What factors may prevent you from being successful? (Lack of agreement on the goal or plan; lack of resources; unforeseen events)
3. How often will you review your progress toward the goal?

<u>Materials Required</u>:

Flipcharts

<u>Approximate Time Required</u>:

40-60 minutes

<u>Source</u>:

Unknown

Pick Your Boss/Subordinate

Objective:

To illustrate the relevant and irrelevant criteria that we use to judge people for leadership and followership positions.

Procedure:

Allow group members to learn at least a minimal amount of information about each other through one or more introduction exercises. Then ask each participant to designate, on a card, their choice of the person they think would make the best boss. On a separate card, ask the participants to select the person who they think would make the best subordinate.

Then ask them to turn over each card and list the characteristics they used to select the boss and subordinate. Then collect the cards and tally the votes for the persons selected. Report the most-chosen bosses (top three) and most-chosen subordinates (top three). Then tabulate and report (or solicit through discussion) the two sets of characteristics used.

Discussion Questions:

    1. How did you feel when you were chosen (or not chosen) as boss or subordinate?
    2. Was there a difference between the characteristics used to select a boss and a subordinate? Why or why not?
    3. Were the characteristics that were used valid or irrelevant? How should we select the ideal boss or subordinate?

Materials Required:

3 x 5 cards

Approximate Time Required:

20 minutes, plus tabulation time

Source:

Kjell R. Knudson

Playing Detective

<u>Objectives</u>:

To vividly illustrate:

    a. The importance of astutely observing an environment.
    b. The degree to which we make inferences from limited data.
    c. The difference between observation and inference.

<u>Procedure</u>:

This procedure is best used at the very beginning of a seminar or program before the trainees have had a substantial opportunity to gather much data. The trainer simply asks the participants (either through direct group discussion or through previous individual responses on paper) to state all the things they "know" about the trainer. These are listed on flipcharts, chalkboard, etc. After these are adequately collected, the trainer then asks the group to generate all the <u>inferences</u> they have made about the trainer thus far. These are recorded on a separate list.

The trainer may then invite the group to comment on the items produced (e.g., are any of the inferences really more like facts? Are any of the facts more like inferences? Why does some confusion exist?). The trainer should then direct the group toward a series of points such as the following:

    1. The group "knew" a lot more about the trainer than any one person did (i.e., more facts were already available than there were first believed to be).
    2. Careful attention to our surroundings can help us learn to acquire (or recognize) more data than we might otherwise have.
    3. We often infer a lot about people from very limited first impressions; these inferences may not be valid until examined.
    4. We often act upon our inferences, but believe we are acting on the basis of facts.
    5. The processes of making accurate observations and astute inferences are quite different, and should be consciously separated in our minds.

<u>Alternatives</u>:

    1. A set of items can be prepared in advance and presented to the trainees on a handout, with two blank columns labelled "Facts" and "Inferences." The trainees can then be asked to assess each item as one or the other (or neither) and the discussion can continue from there.
    2. A highly relevant reference (requiring about 5-10 minutes to present) is a powerful addition to the exercise. Drawn from Sir

Arthur Conan Doyle's <u>Sign of the Four</u>, it tells the tale of Sherlock Holmes baffling Watson by weaving an accurately detailed inferential family history by accurately interpreting the characteristics of a pocket watch.

<u>Discussion Questions</u>:

    1. Why did the observations (and inferences) differ among group members?
    2. Why are first impressions often inaccurate?
    3. How can we improve upon our observation and inference skills?

<u>Materials Required</u>:

None

<u>Approximate Time Required</u>:

15-20 minutes

<u>Source</u>:

Unknown

Knowing vs. Doing

Objective:

To assist in the identification of training vs. non-training problems.

Procedure:

Direct the participants to draw a mental image of an employee they know who is not performing adequately. With their limited knowledge of the facts available, ask them to select an intersection point in the following matrix that best portrays their answers to the two questions on the vertical and horizontal axes dealing with knowledge and attitude. Ask for four volunteers--one each who placed their problem in the four different quadrants. Then explain how such analysis might provide clues to four different solutions:

    1. Quadrant A: If the employee has sufficient job knowledge but has an improper attitude, this may be classed as a motivational problem. The consequences (rewards) of the person's behavior will need to be adjusted.
    2. Quadrant B: If the employee has both job knowledge and a favorable attitude, but performance is unsatisfactory, then the problem may be out of the control of the employee. Conceivably, resources are lacking, time pressures are too severe, or other interferences are constraining behavior. An environmental analysis is called for.
    3. Quadrant C: If the employee lacks both job knowledge and the proper attitude, that person may be improperly placed in the position. This may imply a problem with employee selection, and suggest that transfer or discharge should be considered.
    4. Quadrant D: If the employee desires to perform, but lacks the requisite job knowledge or skills, then additional training may be the answer.

Discussion Questions:

    1. How does the definition of a performance problem impact upon the general strategy for solving it? (See four quadrants, only one of which points clearly to training.)
    2. Considering the employee performance problems in the company, is there any pattern to the form they take (e.g., are most in Quadrant A?)?
    3. What implications does this model have for the role of a trainer as a problem-solver? (e.g., the trainer should help managers identify the type of problems they have and then sometimes steer them away from training)

Materials Required:

The matrix found on the following page, on handout or visual display.

Approximate Time Required:

10-20 minutes

Source:

Attributed to Fred Margolis

Problem Analysis Worksheet

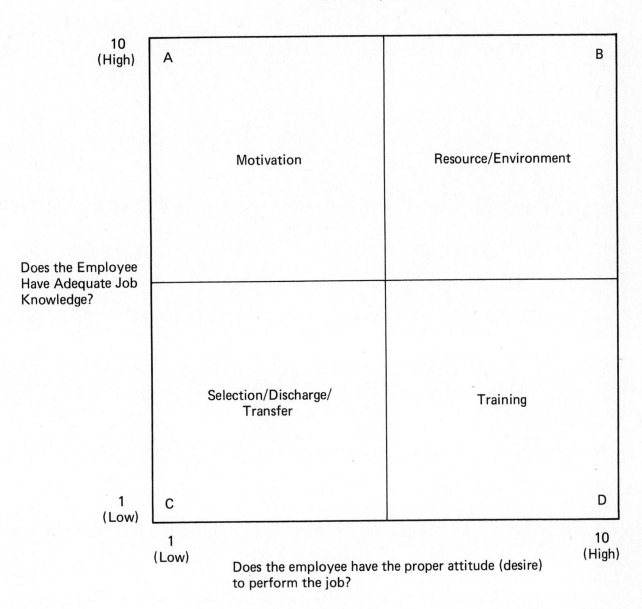

10
(High)

A

Motivation

B

Resource/Environment

Does the Employee
Have Adequate Job
Knowledge?

Selection/Discharge/
Transfer

Training

1
(Low)

C

D

1
(Low)

10
(High)

Does the employee have the proper attitude (desire)
to perform the job?

33

Idea Exchange

Objective:

To encourage participation and sharing of ideas (see also Dollar Exchange).

Procedure:

Each participant is given play money bills (or 3 x 5 cards) which are either mailed out in advance or distributed the day before the first session. They are told to write a single idea on each bill, for a total of five of the best ideas (preferably organized around a single issue or problem, such as, "How to handle a problem trainee."). Names are signed, and they are told that the ideas will be competitively judged and shared.

At the first session, the bills/cards are collected and shuffled in a box. Each attendee draws five bills/cards (not their own) and selects the one believed to be the best, signs their name below that of the idea's originator, and forwards it to the trainer. All of these double nominees are then read aloud and audience reaction may be assessed by a show of hands on a five- or ten-point scale (judged anonymously). After all the ideas have been assessed, the top three (or five) qualify for prizes, which are awarded to both the originator and nominator. The rest of the group also "wins" by virtue of being exposed to a large number of successful ideas.

Alternative Procedure:

All items could be mailed or passed in, and a tabulation (on flip-chart or by handout) prepared and displayed (or distributed) for easier evaluation and better retention.

Discussion Questions:

1. What useful <u>content</u> has been gained? (dependent on the problem/issue posed)
2. What useful <u>process</u> transpired? (widespread participation, a spirit of cooperation and cohesion, etc.)
3. How would the same technique be used on the job? (ask employees for safety ideas, work simplification suggestions, job enrichment approaches, etc.)

Materials Required:

Cards, tickets, or play money

Approximate Time Required:

Up to 1 hour, depending on group size and the elaborateness of discussion and evaluation procedures.

Source:

Successful Meetings, December, 1975.

36

II
CLIMATE SETTING AND ICEBREAKERS

Getting Acquainted

Objective:

To enable first-time attendees in a training session to become acquainted with other participants; to help build a climate of friendliness and informality.

Procedure:

Each person is given a blank name tag and asked to put his or her first name or nickname on it. Then they are asked to list five words or brief phrases that tell something about themselves that can be used as conversation starters. Examples could be home states, hobbies, children, etc. An illustration follows:

Mary (Freckles)
1. Arizona resident
2. Wisconsin native
3. Football nut
4. Jogger
5. Disco enthusiast

After giving the group enough time (about 5 minutes) to write down their 5 items, have them start mixing around in groups of 2-3 (maximum). Every few minutes, tell the group to "change partners" in order to encourage everyone to meet as many new people as possible.

Discussion Questions:

1. Was this exercise helpful to you in getting to know some other people?
2. What kinds of items made the greatest impact on you?
3. How do you now feel about your involvement in this group?

Materials Required:

Blank stick-on name tags

Approximate Time Required:

Flexible, depending on group size. Minimum time 15 minutes.

Source:

Unknown

Getting Acquainted

<u>Objective</u>:

To allow participants to become acquainted through a structured exercise.

<u>Procedure</u>:

At the opening session of a group meeting, each individual is given a blank name tag. Each person completes the following items:

    1. My name is _____.

    2. I have a question about _____
        _____.

    3. I can answer a question about _____
        _____.

After being given a few minutes to respond to the statements, allow 10-15 minutes in which the group is encouraged to meet and mix with as many people as possible.

<u>Materials Required</u>:

Blank name tags

<u>Approximate Time Required</u>:

15-20 minutes, depending on the size of the group.

<u>Source</u>:

Unknown

Camouflage for a Departure

Objective:

To ensure that attendees selecting a concurrent session of a large conference are in the "right" session, and to allow conferees a chance to quickly get acquainted with other attendees.

Procedure:

At large conferences, the program description for individual sessions may not always accurately describe what the speaker and/or content will actually cover. Once the session is started, the attendees may discover the session is not what they thought it was going to be, but still may be reluctant to leave. This method, properly employed, will alleviate that situation.

At the very start of the session, the speaker paraphrases the description in the program book, the session objectives, and briefly indicates precisely what the session is actually going to cover. The speaker then asks everyone in the audience to stand and make 3-4 new acquaintances in the next 2-3 minutes. Just before this brief stand-up period, the speaker acknowledges, "there may be some people in the room who now realize this session may not cover what they thought it would. Since it may be awkward or uncomfortable to get up and leave, let's all stand now, meet some new people, and those of you who want to excuse yourselves can do so easily."

Materials Required:

None

Approximate Time Required:

5 minutes

Source:

Unknown

The Mystery Person

<u>Objective</u>:

To encourage newcomers and "oldtimers" to make new acquaintances and get them to mix with other participants.

<u>Procedure</u>:

At larger conferences or meetings, the new attendee is often left alone and may have difficulty in getting acquainted. The established cliques are hard to crack and the first-time attendee may feel completely <u>apart</u> <u>from</u>--rather than <u>a</u> <u>part</u> <u>of</u>--the group.

To encourage all participants to be more friendly with everyone, designate (in advance and secretly) someone as Mr. or Ms. Mystery Person. Prior to--and during--the first few sessions, promote the exercise by publicizing, "Shake hands with the Mystery Person. He (she) will give you $1." (or every 10th person gets $5, etc.)

Properly publicized, this exercise can be both fun and rewarding. It is especially useful for breaking the ice and creating a warm and friendly atmosphere.

<u>Discussion Questions</u>:

    1. Why are we reluctant to meet new people? (Each new encounter is a challenge to "sell" ourselves and learn about others)
    2. What was the impact of a possible cash incentive on your behavior? (Met more people; talked with them only superficially)
    3. What are some useful conversation-openers that can help us overcome our reticence?

<u>Materials Required</u>:

Cash prizes

<u>Approximate Time Required</u>:

As desired

<u>Source</u>:

Louise Bowker, <u>Meetings and Conventions</u>, October, 1975.

Bingo Game

<u>Objective</u>:

To subtly force newcomers to make new acquaintances in a non-threatening climate.

<u>Procedure</u>:

Using prepared bingo-type cards or sheets (see sample on following page), each person is asked to move around the room until they find a person who fits the description shown. That person then signs his or her name in the appropriate slot.

<u>Materials Required</u>:

Bingo cards (1 for each person)

<u>Approximate Time Required</u>:

20 minutes

<u>Source</u>:

Unknown

BINGO GAME

DIRECTIONS:
Each blank space identifies something about the people in this _____ (seminar, meeting, session, etc.). Seek out your fellow participants and if one of the listed items pertains to them, ask them to sign their names in the appropriate place on your Bingo card. (Even though more than one item may be relevant to any person, only one blank spot should be signed.)

PLAYS TENNIS	IS WEARING RED	SOCCER	CHAPTER OFFICER	HAS GRANDCHILDREN
_____	_____	_____	_____	_____
DRIVES A SPORTS CAR	HATES FOOTBALL	LOVES FOOTBALL	FLIES A PLANE	SPEAKS FOREIGN LANGUAGE
_____	_____	_____	_____	_____
PLAYS PIANO	HAS TROPICAL FISH	FREE	SKIS	COMMITTEE CHAIRPERSON
_____	_____		_____	_____
HAS RED HAIR	HATES SPINACH	HAS 2 CHILDREN	LIKES CAMPING	HAS ATTENDED _____ NATIONAL CONFERENCE
_____	_____	_____	_____	_____
FIRST TIME ATTENDEE	DRIVES PICKUP	BROWN EYES	READS NEWSWEEK	VISITED FOREIGN COUNTRY
_____	_____	_____	_____	_____

Scavenger Hunt

Objective:

To quickly immerse group members into a task-oriented activity so they can begin developing a team identity and initial cohesiveness.

Procedure:

This exercise works best, (a) where it is desirable to form groups for later meaningful task assignments, and (b) when it is obvious the participants would benefit from "loosening up." Divide the group into teams of 4-6 (with a prearranged assignment if they are to work in the same team later on, random assignments if only general social mixing is desired). Give them a specific time period for completing their task, and a minimal set of rules to follow (e.g., they must stay within certain physical boundaries, they must not sabotage other teams). Then provide them with matched lists of objects to obtain (for example: a 1969 penny, a clover blossom, a live ant, a roll of bath tissue, an automobile license plate, a dollar bill with a full-house poker hand represented in the serial number, etc.) It is best to include items that are feasible to obtain, but which may require either ingenuity or collaborative effort within the group to accomplish the task. Score the groups based on the number of items obtained, and announce the winning group (and award them with a possible prize).

Alternative Procedure:

Assign the group the unstructured task of defining and assembling all of the objects, data, or ideas they feel will be useful to them as they engage in their regular learning tasks over the remainder of the training period. Then have each group present and rationalize their findings at the end of the time limit.

Discussion Questions:

    1. How did the group organize to conduct its task (e.g., with individuals assigned to specific items, or as pairs, or with everybody trying to do everything)?
    2. How was this method chosen (e.g., we thought it over and decided it was best, or we just jumped in and began the task)?
    3. How successful was it?
    4. What will you do differently when you are now assigned a more serious learning task (e.g., a case study) as a group?

Materials Required:

A previously-developed list of items (note that the number of copies provided - one or more - to each group might also serve as a contributing factor to various group approaches).

Approximate Time Required:

30-60 minutes, plus discussion

Source:

Unknown

52

Trainee Pictures

Objective:

To help the trainer (and other trainees) learn the names of group members.

Procedure:

Take each registrant's picture at the time they first register for the training program. This is most useful in those extended sessions (3- or 5-day) where participants attend a get-acquainted social session on the previous evening. Using a quick-developing camera, write the name of the individual in the margin or on the reverse side of the picture. The entire set of pictures can then be reviewed prior to the first work session. This allows the trainer to gain name-face familiarity with group members much more rapidly than otherwise possible. It is particularly useful in those settings (e.g., side-arm chairs) where the use of tent cards for names is impractical.

Alternatives:

　　1. Affix the entire set of pictures on a large poster board. Include trainee names and relevant data (e.g., company unit or job/ title) beside each. Place the display near the entry door or at the refreshment table where group members can conveniently study it.
　　2. Hire a local caricature artist to create humorous interpretations of each group member (and the training staff) before the first session and post them conspicuously. Since these often capture a significant facial or personality characteristic, they can be equally useful for facilitating the memorization of names and faces. They can also be distributed at the end of the last session as a special "graduation" gift.

Materials Required:

An instant-developing camera and film.

Approximate Time Required:

15 scattered minutes, depending on the size of the group and the speed of the photographer.

Source:

Various, including Gordon Inskeep (Arizona State University) and Mark Hammer and Leroy Johnson (Washington State University).

Introduction by Association

Objective:

To aid group members in recalling each others' names.

Procedure:

Tell the participants that they will be asked to introduce themselves to the group by standing up, stating their names, and assoc-
iating their names with some item they would bring with them on a
picnic (or other activity). Examples:

>   "My name is Mable, and I'd bring a table."
>   "My name is Dan, and I'd drive a van."
>   "My name is Fred, and I'd bring the bread."
>   "My name is Walt, and I'd bring the salt."
>   "My name is Kay, and I'd bring the insect spray."

Alternative Procedure:

You can ask each group member to select a personal characteristic
that helps identify themself, and do so by rhyme or alliteration,
such as:

>   "I'm Dan, the Macho Man."
>   "I'm Easy Ed."
>   "I'm Jovial Joe."
>   "I'm Sue, with eyes of blue."

Discussion Questions:

How can the principle of association be used to help trainees learn
(remember) other (more important) elements of technical knowledge
in our training program? (General Answer: By either providing them
with old concepts they can associate new ones with, or by stimula-
ting trainees to identify their own relevant associations for the
new ideas.)

Materials Required:

None

Approximate Time Required:

Dependent on group size

Source:

Unknown

56

Who Are You?

Objective:

To enable participants to become acquainted with one another in an
informal setting.

Procedure:

Individuals are instructed to jot down three questions that they
would like to ask a person whom they are just meeting. Suggest
they be creative and not ask the more obvious questions (name,
organization, etc.).

After allowing 3-5 minutes, ask the participants to start moving
around, exchanging questions and answers. Encourage the group to
meet as many new people as possible.

Reassemble the entire group and have all persons introduce themselves. As each individual is introduced, other participants are
encouraged to add other pieces of information or details shared
earlier. This will eventually provide a highly enriched composite
picture of each participant.

Discussion Questions:

    1. What were some of the more interesting things discovered
about people? Would they have been uncovered in "normal" cocktail
party conversations? Why not?
    2. What were some of the more productive questions asked?
    3. What questions proved to be less productive? Why?

Materials Required:

None

Approximate Time Required:

30 minutes, depending on group size

Source:

Unknown

Preconceived Ideas and Fears

Objective:

To allow participants to express, share, and reduce the misconceptions they may have brought with them to a training program.

Procedure:

In some seminars and workshops, participants may be drawn from a large geographical area, may know very little about the prospective program, may not know each other, or may not know what comprises expected trainee behavior. Consequently, a forum for exchanging some preconceptions may be appropriate.

Form the members into small groups of 4-6 persons. Have each group select a recorder (a flipchart or notepaper should be provided). Ask them to quickly respond to the question, "What fears, concerns, or preconceived notions did you have prior to coming here today (tonight)?" After a brief response-gathering period, ask the reporters to present their lists to the entire group. This will present excellent opportunities for the trainer to empathize with trainee needs, as well as provide reassurance and support by using the items to indicate how the seminar does/does not relate to those concerns.

Discussion Questions:

1. What were some of the fears/concerns/notions expressed in each group?
   (Prior examples include the following)

   "Will I be the oldest (youngest) person?"
   "Will I act appropriately at my first professional seminar?"
   "I'm sure everyone will be more experienced than I am."
   "Will they be more (less) casually dressed than I am?"
   "Will everyone speak in acronyms and abbreviations?"
   "What will I get out of the program?"
   "What kind of questions should I ask?"
   "What will the room/program/trainers, etc., be like?"

2. What can we (as trainers) do to diminish those concerns? (e.g., explain the dress "code," define all acronyms used, solicit questions, etc.)

Materials Required:

Flipcharts or notepaper

Approximate Time Required:

20-30 minutes

Source:

Unknown

Roles of a Good Trainee

Objective:

To create a constructive climate for discussion in a training session.

Procedure:

In many groups of entry-level trainees, the participants have previously attended no (or very few) formal training programs. Therefore, it is often helpful to establish clear norms for what constitutes acceptable (productive) trainee behavior.

One approach to accomplish this quickly and with a certainty of hitting the "right" rules is to present (orally, by handout, or by overhead transparency) a set of pre-developed guidelines for behaviors that trainees would ideally engage in or avoid. This has the advantage of clarity, but has the potential danger of creating a limiting, rule-filled environment. Presented in a positive manner, however, the authors have had considerable success with the use of a handout (such as the example found on the next page), especially when it is "spiced up" with some humorous illustrations.

Alternative Procedures:

    1. Engage the group (early in the session) in a discussion of the productive and nonproductive behaviors they have seen (or can think of) on the part of seminar participants. This has the value of involving them in the creation of their own norms for their behavior.
    2. One organization has prepared printed tent cards for participants' names, with five rules of appropriate seminar behavior on the back side. While the name faces outward to the trainer and other trainees, the rules are visually present to the trainee at all times as a constant reminder.

Materials Required:

Possible handout, transparency, or tent cards

Approximate Time Required:

5-10 minutes

Source:

Unknown

Suggestions for Effective Seminar Participation

<u>DO</u>

Ask a question when you have one

Feel free to share an illustration

Request an example if a point is not clear

Search for ways in which you can apply a general principle or idea to your work

Think of ways you can pass on ideas to your subordinates

Be skeptical - don't buy <u>everything</u> you hear

<u>DON'T</u>

Try to develop an extreme problem just to prove the leader doesn't have all the answers (the leader doesn't)

Close your mind by saying, "This is all fine in theory,
but..."

Assume that all topics covered will be equally relevant
to your needs

Take extensive notes - the handouts will satisfy most of
your needs

ESP Ice-Breaker

<u>Objective</u>:

To use a quick demonstration to attract and focus the group's attention on you and the presentation to follow.

<u>Procedure</u>:

Ask for a volunteer to assist you. Explain that you are going to foretell the results of an arithmetic exercise by the virtue of ESP, Extra Sensory Perception. Position yourself any place where you <u>cannot</u> see what the person is going to write. Ask the volunteer to <u>write</u> on the flipchart, chalkboard, etc., any 3-digit number. (note: The number must <u>not</u> be a mirror image, e.g., 323.) Then <u>tell</u> the person to reverse the number and subtract the lower number from the higher one; for example:

$$\begin{array}{r} 821 \\ -128 \\ \hline 693 \end{array}$$

Now reverse this number and add it to the preceding product to obtain:

$$\begin{array}{r} 693 \\ 396 \\ \hline 1089 \end{array}$$

As the volunteer completes the calculation, hold up a prepared card on which you had previously written the number 1089. (<u>Note</u>: This exercise will <u>always</u> result in the number 1089.) On occasion, the initial subtraction will yield a 2-digit number. For example:

$$\begin{array}{r} 786 \\ -687 \\ \hline 99 \end{array}$$

In such a case, simply direct the volunteer to add a zero in front (99 changes to 099). Proceed as earlier indicated:

$$\begin{array}{r} 099 \\ \text{Reverse it to} \quad 990 \quad \text{and the} \\ \hline \text{result again is} \quad 1089 \end{array}$$

<u>Materials Required</u>:

Chalkboard, or flipchart and prepared large display card

<u>Approximate Time Required</u>:

3 minutes

<u>Source</u>: Unknown

The National Trainers' Test

Objective:

To humorously self-assess one's expertise as a trainer.

Procedure:

In a light way, tell the group you are going to administer the National Trainers' Test. (Note: The title and questions can be easily changed to fit the particular group.) Have each person place their right hand on a flat surface with fingers outstretched, making certain the knuckles on the second (middle) finger stay tightly on the flat surface.

Advise the group that you are going to ask four simple questions. If the answer is "Yes," they are to respond by raising the thumb or finger as you so indicate.

    1. "Start with your thumb. Are you involved in training?" (If yes, raise the right thumb high.)
    2. "OK, thumb down. Now for the 'pinkie.' Do you have an interesting job?" (If so, raise the smallest finger.)
    3. "OK, now for the forefinger or index finger. Do you enjoy what you're doing?" (If so, raise the forefinger.)
    4. "Thank you. Now with thumb and fingers in their original position, here's the last question. Using the ring finger, and please be honest with us, are you really any good at your job?" (If so, raise your ring finger.)

The quick laughter will indicate that if the participants held their knuckles and other fingers down, it is practically impossible to raise their ring finger.

Materials Required:

None

Approximate Time Required:

5 minutes

Source:

Unknown

The Dollar Exchange/Idea Exchange

Objective:

To encourage a climate for open exchange of ideas among participants.

Procedure:

Ask for the loan of a dollar from a member of the group. Displaying
it prominently in one hand, proceed to ask for the loan of a second
dollar from another trainee. Then carefully repay the first loaner
with the second dollar and repay the second loaner with the first
dollar. Then ask the rhetorical question, "Is either of these persons now richer than they were before?" (Neither, of course, is.)
Then point out to the group that by contrast had two ideas been
shared as readily, not only the respective givers, but all participants, would be richer in experience than they were previously.

Alternative:

Give each participant one (or more) pieces of pre-printed play money.
Let them exchange the money first to experience the lack of enrichment that ensues. Then let each person write an idea on the play
money and either circulate the bills, or post them in a conspicuous
place where members may inspect them at their leisure (during coffee
breaks).

Discussion Questions:

   1.   What factors prevent us from sharing useful ideas and
insights with others?
   2.   What forces encourage us to share ideas with others in
training seminars?

Materials Required:

None, under the first procedure. Play money under the alternative.

Approximate Time Required:

5-10 minutes

Source:

Unknown

The Pike (Hot Stove) Syndrome

Objective:

To illustrate to trainees that the limits to their use of the
training content lie within themselves as much as externally.

Procedure:

Relate the story of the northern pike, placed in one-half of a
large aquarium, with numerous minnows unavailable to it in the
other half of the glass-divided tank. The hungry pike makes numerous efforts to obtain the minnows, but only succeeds in battering
itself against the glass, finally learning that reaching the
minnows is an impossible task. The glass plate partition is then
removed, but the pike does not attack the minnows. The same pattern
of behavior can be viewed in a cat that jumps onto a hot stove
(once!). The subsequent behavior of the pike and cat demonstrates
the Pike Syndrome, characterized by:

1. Ignoring Differences
2. Assumption of Complete Knowledge
3. Overgeneralized Reactions
4. Rigid Commitment to the Past
5. Refusal to Consider Alternatives
6. Inability to Function Under Stress

Discussion Questions:

1. What are some examples where people you know have exhibited
the Pike Syndrome?
2. How can we help others (or ourselves) break out of it?
3. In what ways is it useful?

Materials Required:

None

Approximate Time Required:

5-10 minutes

Sources:

Eden Ryl, Ramic Productions' film entitled "Grab Hold of Today."

The Zen Koan (A Cup of Tea)

Objective:

To open trainee minds to possibilities of new learning.

Procedure:

At the beginning of a training program, relate the following tale to the participants. It is a Zen Buddhist Koan - a centuries-old meaningful story about life.

A Cup of Tea

Nan-in, a Japanese master, received a university professor who came to inquire about Zen. They chatted a while. Nan-in then served tea. He poured his visitor's cup full, and then kept pouring. The professor watched the overflow until he could no longer restrain himself. "It is overfull. No more will go in," he exclaimed.

"Like this cup," Nan-in said, "you are full of your own judgments, opinions, and speculations. How can I show you Zen until you empty your first cup?"

Alternatives:

1. Wait to tell the story until a participant emerges as a "know-it-all" who has heard it all before, and then use it as a parable for the entire group. (This requires greater skill, and may risk offending at least one person.)
2. Instead of telling the story by narration, arrange the props as listed below and have an accomplice (a fellow team trainer or by prearrangement with a trainee) help you in role-playing the vignette. If presented properly, the additional realism can have great impact on the participants.

Discussion Questions:

1. How does this relate to our training program?
2. Who has experienced being the Zen master? The student? How did it feel?
3. What basic concepts are being emphasized in this role?

Materials (Optional):

Cup, saucer, coffee (or tea, or water), and a tray to catch the overflow.

Time Required:

5 minutes

Source:

Reps, P., _Zen Flesh_, _Zen Bones_ (New York: Anchor), 1961, p. 27.

Brainteasers

Objective:

To provide a quick, fun exercise that will facilitate the interaction of strangers and their formation into task-oriented groups.

Procedure:

This is strictly a "for fun" exercise and should be introduced as
such. It purports simply to give participants a chance to do some
liberal translation by interpreting visual and written communications.

Form the members into small groups of 3-4 persons each. Tell them
that they have 5 minutes to decipher the 20 brainteasers found on
the following page into a word or brief phrase. (The team with
the highest score may be promised a prize.)

Answers:

1. Sandbox
2. Man Overboard
3. I Understand
4. Reading Between the Lines
5. Long Underwear
6. Cross Roads
7. Down Town
8. Tri-cycle
9. Bi-level
10. 3 Degrees Below Zero
11. Knee on Lights
12. Circles Under the Eyes
13. High Chair
14. Paradise
15. Touchdown
16. 6 Feet Under Ground
17. Mind Over Matter
18. He's Beside Himself
19. Backwards Glance
20. Life After Death

Materials Required:

Brainteasers as shown, on a handout or overhead transparency

Approximate Time Required:

10 minutes

Source: Unknown

75

BRAIN TEASERS

1.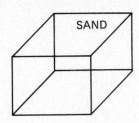

2. MAN
BOARD

3. STAND
I

4. READING

5. WEAR
LONG

6. ROAD
A
D

7. T
O
W
N ∨

8. CYCLE
CYCLE
CYCLE

9. LE
VEL

10. 0
──────
M. D
B. A.
PH. D

11. KNEE
────
LIGHT

12. i i
0 0
0 0
0 0
0 0

13. CHAIR

14.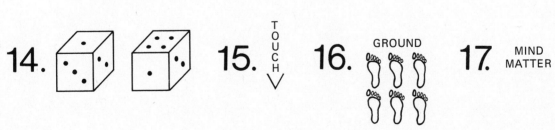

15. T
O
U
C
H ∨

16. GROUND

17. MIND
MATTER

18. HE'S / HIMSELF

19. ECNALG

20. DEATH   LIFE

77

The Argument of Obviousness

Objective:

To point out that common sense is not so common.

Procedure:

Ask the group to generate a series of widely-held generalizations about human behavior (or some other relevant topic). Examples might be, "All _____ are lazy;" "No one ever does _____;" "Only _____ people can be effective managers;" "The only way to motivate people is to _____." Post these statements conspicuously. Highlight (with color, or by underlining) the key words of "all," "every," "always," "never," "only," etc.

If possible, obtain and read aloud the brief but potent tale told by Paul Lazarsfeld in the reference below. He pointed out the need for testing (and possible confirmation)of everyday statements that we commonly take for granted, and concluded that "something is wrong with the entire argument of obviousness."

After discussion of the questions below, review the statements generated earlier for their basis in fact.

Discussion Questions:

    1. How do people acquire such grossly incorrect beliefs?
    2. What is the behavioral impact of holding such beliefs?
    3. How can we better prevent the development of such attitudes?
    4. How can we recognize such "obvious" statements after we hear them?

Materials Required:

None

Approximate Time Required:

15 minutes

Source:

Expository Review of the American Soldier (1949), pp. 379-80. As quoted and expanded in E. F. Jones & H. B. Gerard, Foundations of Social Psychology (New York: Wiley, 1967), pp. 34-5.

III
PRESENTATION

Overcoming Trainer Fears

Objective:

To recognize fear of public speaking as being normal, and to offer suggestions for its resolution.

Procedure:

This exercise can be useful with new trainers, with part-time trainers who need improved platform skills, or with any personnel who will be asked to make in-house or public presentations. Begin by asking the group, "What do you believe are the greatest fears of most people in our country?" Briefly note the responses on a chalkboard or flipchart. Ask if there is any consensus regarding the single greatest fear. Then present the hypothetical list illustrated on the following page. Point out that, if the information is indeed valid, many other persons share the group's concern over the challenge of making effective presentations or leading productive training sessions. Then ask the group to recall, or brainstorm, all the ways in which a trainer might prevent or overcome such fears. These items should again be displayed prominently so that participants have adequate opportunity to take notes if they choose.

Alternative Procedures:

1. Either as a guide to the discussion, or as a way to achieve closure, a handout such as the "Suggestions for Overcoming Fear of Speaking Before a Group" may be distributed.

2. If the group is large, it may be divided into small (five-person) buzz groups for brief time periods and asked to generate at least five good suggestions from each.

Materials Required:

Possible transparency of list of fears, and handout of "Suggestions".

Approximate Time Required:

15 minutes and more, depending on the depth of discussion desired.

Source:

Unknown

The Ten Worst Human Fears (in the U.S.)*

1. Speaking before a group

2. Heights

3. Insects and bugs

4. Financial problems

5. Deep water

6. Sickness

7. Death

8. Flying

9. Loneliness

10. Dogs

*David Wallechinsky et al.: The Book of Lists
(New York: Wm. Morrow & Co., Inc., 1977)

Suggestions for Overcoming Fear of Speaking before a Group

1. Know the material well (be an expert).
2. Practice your presentation (pilot-test, and possibly video-tape yourself).
3. Use involvement techniques (participation).
4. Learn participants' names and use them.
5. Establish your credibility early.
6. Use eye contact to establish rapport.
7. Take a course in public speaking.
8. Exhibit your advance preparation (via handouts, etc.).
9. Anticipate potential problems (and prepare probable responses).
10. Check in advance the facilities and AV equipment.
11. Obtain information about the group in advance (through observation or questionnaire).
12. Convince yourself to relax (breathe deeply; meditate; talk to yourself).
13. Prepare an outline and follow it.
14. Manage your appearance (dress comfortably and appropriately).
15. Rest up so that you are physically and psychologically alert.
16. Use your own style (don't imitate someone else).
17. Use your own words (don't read).
18. Put yourself in your trainees' shoes (they're asking, "What's in it for me?").
19. Assume they are on your side (they aren't necessarily antagonistic or hostile).
20. Provide an overview of the presentation (state the end objectives).
21. Accept some fears as being good (energizing stress vs. destructive).
22. Introduce yourself to the group in advance (via a social context).
23. Identify your fears, categorize them as controllable or uncontrollable, and confront them.
24. Give special emphasis to the first five minutes (super-preparation).
25. Image yourself as a good speaker (self-fulfilling prophecy).
26. Practice responses to tough questions or situations.
27. Create an informal setting (sit on a table).

Waiting to Get Started

Objectives:

    1. To convey to the participants the instructor's enthusiasm for the training task at hand.
    2. To stimulate the trainees to unleash their energies toward the training program.

Procedure:

Obtain a cover from each of the three magazines mentioned below. Display them prominently at the appropriate points in the following story.

    As we start today's opening session, I'd like to tell you the story of the 3 little boys waiting in the doctor's office for their shots.
    The doctor went up to the first one, who was reading <u>Popular Mechanics</u>, and said, "Johnny, what are you going to be when you grow up?"
    Immediately, Johnny said, "I'm going to be a mechanic. I want to fix autos and make airplanes fly."
    The doctor then went up to Tommy, who was reading <u>Sports Afield</u>. "Tommy, what are you going to be?"
    Tommy, without hesitation, said, "I want to be a hunting and fishing guide. Yes, that's what I want to be."
    The doctor then went over to little redheaded, freckle-faced Billy, who was reading <u>Playboy Magazine</u> carefully. When asked the same question, Billy thought for a moment and then said slowly, "I don't know what you call it, but I can hardly wait to get started."

Discussion Questions:

    1. Is everybody here today as ready and willing to begin as little Billy was?
    2. What factors made Billy so motivated? (Clear objective, unfulfilled need, potential reward, etc.)
    3. How can we motivate our trainees/employees so that they can "hardly wait to get started?" (Same suggestion as in #2)

Materials Required:

Three magazine covers

Approximate Time Required:

5-10 minutes

Source: Unknown

89

The Dumb Joke

Objective:

To encourage participants to ask (dumb) questions.

Procedure:

Relate the following story to the group (straight-faced).

"Have you heard the one about the graduate student who was doing a study? He had a cockroach and he set it on a table and told the cockroach to jump. And it jumped to the end of the table. The student picked the cockroach up and pulled off a couple of legs. Then he set it back down and told it to jump. The cockroach jumped about halfway down the table. The student picked it up and pulled off a couple more legs and set it down. He then told the cockroach to jump and it just jumped a little ways. Then the student picked it up and pulled off the cockroach's last two legs and set it down. He told the cockroach to jump and it didn't move. So the student concluded that a cockroach with no legs is deaf."

Told properly, the joke will (at best) obtain groans from your audience.

Discussion Questions:

    1. "Why would I tell a dumb joke like that?" (to loosen up the audience)
    2. "What lessons are there for you in that incident?" (no one should be afraid to make a "dumb" statement or ask a "stupid" question)

Materials Required:

None

Approximate Time Required:

5-10 minutes

Source:

Cal Green (Training Director at Telxon Corporation, Houston, Texas) as presented at the ICS Showcase Session, ASTD National Conference and Exposition, June 3, 1977.

The Torn Shirt

Objective:

To impress upon your participants that they must ask (good) questions.

Procedure:

Tell the participants the following story:

"I have trouble finding dress shirts in the correct size (e.g., 14½ x 36). Therefore, whenever I travel I always browse in clothing stores to search for some new ones, usually with no success. Recently, I was in New York and dropped into a store. The clerk was very nice. He said, 'Can I help you, sir?' (I liked him already.) He proceeded to ask me a series of well-constructed questions (e.g., 'What characteristics do you demand in a shirt?') I said there were four: correct size, collars that won't wrinkle when stuffed in a suitcase, buttons that won't crack when laundered, and cuffs that won't fray. So he asked me, 'If I can show you shirts like that, will you buy them?' I eagerly answered that I would.

"He brought out a box of shirts, all 14½ x 36 - exactly the right size - and I was intrigued. Then he unwrapped one and proceeded to give it three other tests. First, he twisted the collar between his fists and shook it out - no wrinkles. Then he picked up a hammer and rapped one of the buttons against his desk - no cracks. Then he grabbed a piece of sandpaper and vigorously rubbed a cuff - no fraying. Now I was really impressed, so I immediately bought a dozen of them, even though they cost $18 each (a total of $216).

"As a matter of fact, I'm wearing one of those shirts today." (Proceed to show the group at close range that the collar, cuffs, and buttons are okay.) "And I learned a critical lesson that day - the person who asks the right questions at the right time will not only be in control of the conversation, but learn something also."

Then proceed to shed your suit/sport jacket (and vest) as you casually return to the front of the room, exposing a shirt that has (conveniently) disintegrated into shreds and strips throughout the body and sleeves, while the collar, cuffs, and buttons have remained intact.

Major Points:

1. You will have successfully loosened up your audience through the use of a "true" story with a surprise ending.

93

2. You have brought yourself down to the level of your audience by disclosing that you have been "taken" once in a while.
3. You can impress upon your audience how the eventual problem would not have arisen if you had only asked a few good questions at the time.

Materials Required:

One shirt, cut and ripped to shreds in all places not visible when a jacket and vest are worn.

Approximate Time Required:

Ten minutes.

Source:

Joel Weldon, Scottsdale, Arizona.

Five Easy Questions

<u>Objective</u>:

To demonstrate that (some) behavior is quite predictable.

<u>Procedure</u>:

Ask the participants to take out a sheet of paper and a pen or pencil. Tell them that they will be asked to name four items <u>very</u> quickly in response to four questions. It is their <u>first</u> reaction that is desired. Then <u>quickly</u> ask them:

1. What is your favorite color?
2. Name a piece of furniture.
3. Name a flower.
4. Pick a number from 1-4.
5. Name an animal in a zoo.

Then display the following answers: Red, Chair, Rose, 3, Lion.

<u>Discussion Questions</u>:

1. How many had each item "correct"? (Ask for a show of hands. A surprising number will have chosen these responses.)
2. What does this illustrate to you? (Some human behavior, attitudes, or reactions are predictable. The key is to be an alert observer - see "Playing Detective" - and/or a statistician. A humorous illustration is contained in the story of the person who noted that one-half of the high school seniors in Iowa scored below average on a certain test!)

<u>Materials Required</u>:

None, unless a transparency of the questions and answers is desired.

<u>Approximate Time Required</u>:

5 minutes.

<u>Source</u>:

Eden Ryl, Ramic Productions, Newport Beach, CA 92660

Table Topics

<u>Objective:</u>

To give participants practice in quick response and to allow them a chance to give spontaneous presentations with little preparation time.

<u>Procedure:</u>

This activity can be used in training for oral presentations. A series of 3 x 5 cards is prepared, each card having a word on it (examples are "Learning," "Evaluation," "Objectives," "Visuals," etc.). The trainer then flips over a card and calls on a trainee at random. That person then must stand up and give a 60-second impromptu talk on the assigned topic. This procedure is followed in turn through all (or several) of the participants. The topics, of course, are dependent upon the nature of the seminar. Critiques can also be added if desired.

<u>Discussion Questions:</u>

    1. Nervousness is natural with these on-the-spot assignments. What could we do to alleviate these fears?
    2. Thinking back, what's the first thing that flashed in your mind when your name was called?
    3. What are some mental notes we can make to help "catalogue" or prepare an organized response?

<u>Materials Required:</u>

3 x 5 index cards

<u>Approximate Time Required:</u>

10-15 minutes

<u>Source:</u>

Adapted from a Toastmaster, International exercise

Handling Objections in Sales Training

Objective:

To encourage participants to anticipate objections and be able to respond to them quickly and satisfactorily.

Procedure:

Prepare 3 x 5 index cards on which are noted possible objections encountered in a sales situation. (Leave one side blank.) The participant draws a card from the deck and reads aloud the objection (for example, "I believe your price seems higher than our existing supplier's"). The trainee must then respond spontaneously. A critique follows from the trainer and group in which other possible answers or responses are discussed. Then the deck is rotated to another participant, and the process is repeated.

Alternative:

An alternative way is to give the respondent a moment of preparation before vocally responding. This method may be desirable for novice trainees to help build their confidence before demanding job-like spontaneity.

Discussion Questions:

    1. What are your feelings when put on the spot like this? (Stimulated, fearful) What additional responses can you think of now?
    2. The "Yes, but" or "Yes, and" techniques are valid ones in handling objections. What other methods are pertinent?
    3. Preparation and anticipating objections are key points. How can we better remember some of our standard responses? (Key words, a success/failure experience, etc.)

Materials Required:

3 x 5 cards

Approximate Time Required:

Dependent on the size of the group; minimum 15 minutes

Source:

Ray Higgins, Armour Dial Company

Thinking on Your Feet

Objective:

To encourage quick thinking in a pressure situation.

Procedure:

Similar to the "Handling Objections" exercise, this activity also has a multiplicity of uses. A few volunteers are asked to assist in illustrating the difficulty, but importance, of being able to think quickly on one's feet. As an objection (as in sales training) is voiced, the trainer lights a match and hands it to the trainee. The trainee then must respond to the question or objection before the lighted match burns down or the flame is too close to the fingers. As soon as the response is voiced, the match is extinguished.

Discussion Questions:

    1. Like the threat of that match, what other pressures may cause difficulty in these situations?
    2. Was the group's peer pressure through observation a substantial one?
    3. Are there some dangers also in replying or responding too quickly to objections? If so, what are they?

Materials Required:

Book of matches

Approximate Time Required:

Dependent on the size of the group, 15 minutes minimum

Source:

Unknown

IV
METHODS

The "66" Technique

Objective:

To get a large group actively involved in a discussion session.

Procedure:

The "66" discussion technique allows for small groups to discuss
any type of relevant or pertinent topic. It is a variation of any
typical small group discussion method. It is more structured in
that the total group is divided into 6-person teams. Have each
group identify a recorder. (Note that all groups could have different or similar topics.) After a problem is assigned to each of the
groups, a 6-minute period of time is allowed for the group to talk
about the issue. Tell the group when there are 2 minutes left;
then, with 1 minute left, suggest that the group use the last
minute to wrap things up. Depending on the time available, get
representative reports from as many groups as possible. Have each
group post its report on flipchart paper and physically attach it
to the wall with masking tape.

Discussion Questions:

    1. What did your group conclude?
    2. How do the reports from the various groups compare/
contrast?
    3. What effect did the time limit have on your group's
capacity to generate a meaningful set of responses?

Materials Required:

A room with moveable chairs or table and chair setting; flipcharts.

Approximate Time Required:

15-minute minimum. Time spent is contingent upon the size of the
group and time restraints.

Source:

J. Donald Phillips, "Report on Discussion 66," Adult Education
Journal, 1948, 7, pp. 181-2.

Nominal Group Technique

Objective:

To obtain multiple inputs from several persons on a problem/issue in a structured format.

Procedure:

This technique is a structured variation of small-group discussion methods. The process prevents the domination of discussion by a single person, encourages the more passive persons to participate, and results in a set of prioritized solutions or recommendations.

    1. Divide the persons present into small groups of 5-6 members, preferably seated around a table.
    2. State an open-ended task (e.g., "What are some ways we could encourage employees to car-pool?").
    3. Have each person spend several minutes in silence individually brainstorming all the possible ideas they can generate, and jot these ideas down.
    4. Have the groups collect the ideas by having the ideas shared in round-robin fashion (one response per person each time), while all are recorded in key terms on a flipchart. No criticism is allowed, but clarification in response to questions is encouraged.
    5. Then have each person evaluate the ideas and individually vote for the best ones (e.g., the best idea gets 5 points, the next best 4 points, etc.).
    6. Votes are shared within the group and tabulated. A group report is prepared, showing the ideas receiving the most points.
    7. Allow time for brief group presentations on their conclusions.

Discussion Questions:

    1. What are the advantages of this technique? (Allows voting anonymity; provides opportunity for equal participation of members; eliminates distractions of other group methods, etc.)
    2. What are the disadvantages of this method? (Opinions may not converge in the voting process; cross-fertilization of ideas is constrained; the process may appear mechanical)
    3. For what types of problems/issues do you see this method potentially used?

Materials Required:

A problem, and one flipchart per group.

<u>Approximate Time Required</u>:

30-60 minutes

<u>Source</u>:

A. L. Delbecq and A. H. VandeVen, "A Group Process Model for
Problem Identification and Program Planning," <u>Journal</u> <u>of</u> <u>Applied</u>
<u>Behavioral</u> <u>Science</u>, 1971, 7:4, pp. 466-491.

108

Brainstorming

To give participants an opportunity to engage in a creative problem-solving exercise.

Procedure:

Research indicates that creativity can be cultivated by the use of simple and practical exercise. All too often, however, the spark of innovative thinking is dampened by killer phrases like "We tried it last year," "We've always done it that way," and a host of similar comments.

To acclimate participants by flicking on their innate green light of creativity, a sample brainstorm session should be used. The basic ground rules of brainstorming are:

1. No critical judgment is permitted
2. Free-wheeling is welcomed (i.e., the wilder the idea, the better)
3. Quantity, not quality, is desired
4. Combination and improvement of ideas are sought

With these four basic rules in mind, divide the participants into groups of 4-6 people. Their task for 60 seconds will be to suggest all the ways they can think of for using a paper clip. Have someone in each group merely tally the number of ideas, not necessarily the ideas themselves. At the end of the one minute, ask the groups to report first the number of ideas they generated, and then get a sampling of some of the seemingly "crazy" or "far out" ideas. Suggest that sometimes these "silly" ideas may well turn out to be very workable.

Alternative Method:

The problem may be to think of ways to improve the standard (non-mechanical) lead pencil.

Discussion Questions:

1. What reservations do you have about the technique?
2. What kinds of problems is brainstorming best suited for?
3. What potential applications at work can you see for brainstorming?

Materials Required:

A paper clip for display at each table.

<u>Approximate Time Required</u>:

10 minutes

<u>Source</u>:

Alex Osborn

Delphi Decision Making

Objective:

To demonstrate the value of a structured approach to obtain convergence of opinions in the decision-making (prediction) process.

Procedure:

The Delphi Technique involves the selection of a panel of informed experts, each of whom is genuinely interested in solving the problem at hand. Problems involve the prediction of a future state of affairs (e.g., corporate sales five years from now). Panelists are solicited for their best guesses, feedback (group average and frequency distribution) is provided, and the process is repeated (anonymously) several times. A distinct convergence of thought usually emerges, and can later be shown to be accurate.

The technique can be quickly demonstrated to the group. Fill a jar with popcorn kernels (count them first). Display the jar to the group and ask the members to estimate the number of kernels. Compute the mean, media, and frequency distribution and report it to the group (sometimes the rationales for the conclusions reached are also shared). Iterate the process three times (or until a stable result is obtained). Disclose the correct answer, and ask the group members to compare the accuracy of their initial estimates with the accuracy of the group's final conclusion.

Discussion Questions:

    1. Which was more accurate: the original individual estimates or the final group decision?
    2. Why does the group tend to be more accurate?
    3. Why did the group converge in their answers?
    4. What applications does the Delphi Technique have in your job?

Materials Required:

Jar of popcorn or similar prop

Approximate Time Required:

30 minutes

Source:

Unknown

V
MOTIVATION

Motivation Exercise

Objective:

To illustrate that motivation is internal, but that external incentives can initiate action in humans.

Procedure:

Since motivation is an often maligned subject, stress that the dictionary definition of motivation is something "from within, not without, that prompts or incites an action."

To illustrate, ask the group to "please raise your right hands." Pause a moment, thank the group, and ask them, "Now why did you do that?" The response will be, "Because you asked us to," "Because you said 'please'", etc.

After 3-4 additional responses, say, "OK, now would you please all stand and pick up your chairs?"

In all likelihood, this will get no action. Continue, "If I told you there were some dollar bills scattered around the room under the chairs, would that motivate you to stand and pick up your chairs?" Most still will not move, so say, "Well, let me tell you there are indeed some dollar bills under some chairs." (Ordinarily, two or three participants will rise, and soon most everyone will follow suit. As dollar bills are found, point out, "There's one over here; here's one in front," etc.)

Discussion Questions:

1. Why did it take more effort to "motivate" you the second time?
2. Did the money motivate you? (Stress that money often does not act as a motivator.)
3. What's the only real way to motivate? (Acknowledge any relevant answer, but emphasize the only way to get a person to do something is to make a person want to do it. There is no other way!)

Materials Required:

Several one dollar bills hidden (taped) under participants' chairs.

Approximate Time Required:

10 minutes

Source: Unknown

Positive Reinforcement for the Trainees

Objective:

To demonstrate that positive reinforcement increases the probability that a given behavior will appear again.

Procedure:

Reinforcement theory predicts that if a given behavior is followed by a positive consequence, that behavior will increase in its subsequent frequency. The person in control must make sure the consequences are contingent upon performance, and that the consequences are positive for the recipient.

Joel Weldon has perfected the process in his motivational presentations, and other trainers can borrow directly from his technique. Joel has produced stick-on labels for small cans which say, "Success comes in cans, not in cannots." When hearing the catchy little phrase and viewing the take-home reward that can be theirs for displaying the appropriate behavior, the participants enjoy the exercise and respond accordingly. Whenever a person contributes an insightful comment or breaks up the room with a humorous remark, Joel reinforces that person with a "can," and the remainder of the group tries that much harder to obtain their "cans."

In general, the key is to:

1. Identify something that will be generally desired (e.g., free drink tickets for the cocktail party).
2. Let the group know that these rewards are available (either through prior announcement or after the first appropriate behavior).
3. Give the rewards out liberally, but conditionally.

Discussion Questions:

At the end of the session, a brief presentation can be made on positive reinforcement by focusing the discussion around the following questions:

1. Why did people participate so actively?
2. What would have happened if the trainer had withheld a reward one time?
3. What if the trainer had chosen the wrong reinforcement for the group?
4. What other applications of positive reinforcement can the group see?

<u>Materials Required:</u>

Advance selection of reinforcers (e.g., cans, slogans printed on frisbees, baseball caps, t-shirts, bumper stickers, drink tickets, dollar bills).

<u>Approximate Time Required:</u>

Less than five minutes to introduce; minimal time interspersed within the session.

<u>Source:</u>

Joel H. Weldon, Scottsdale, AZ

Competing for Dollars

Objective:

To utilize competition and economic rewards to stimulate high audience involvement in the learning process.

Procedure:

Select a set of items that a trainee group is to have learned (e.g., the characteristics of a new product or the components of a machine.) List these and other erroneous items on two large display boards, screens, or worksheets. Select two teams of two persons each to work at each board. Their objective is to place an "X" next to each of the correct features. The non-participants are assigned the same task at their regular tables. After a brief period of time, the trainer stops the action.

The boards are then turned toward the audience, who are asked to spot errors on the boards. Members identifying a true error are awarded a silver dollar for each one spotted. Then the winning team members (those with the least errors) are awarded five dollars.

The exercise provides a spirit of competition as well as an achievement opportunity for the participants. It is, in effect, a fun way to "test" an entire group, and the camaraderie that develops often is exemplified by the "winners" buying refreshments for the "losers." Multiple products (and lists) allow repetition of the exercise several times.

Materials Required:

Advance list and display board (hook and loop, magnetic, chalk, etc.)

Approximate Time Required:

15-20 minutes

Source:

Jack Shepman, "Dollars for Errors," Training, April, 1978, pp. 11, 54.

119

What Do People Want from Their Jobs?

Objective:

To give participants an opportunity to discuss what factors motivate employees.

Procedure:

Distribute copies of the form, "What Do People Want From Their Jobs?" Divide the group into subgroups of 3-5 people each. Ask each person to indicate which of the 10 items listed is felt to be of most importance in contributing to employee morale. Weight the items from 1-10, assigning 10 to the most important item, 9 for #2, etc., in a reverse weighting order so that all 10 numbers are used.

Then have each group total the individual weights within their group. Rank the 10 items under the column marked "Group."

Advise the group that this same scale has been given to thousands of workers around the country. In comparing related rankings of both employees and supervisors, the typical supervisory group is ranked in this order (mark in the "Supervisors" column).

    1. High wages
    2. Job Security
    3. Promotion in the company
    4. Good working conditions
    5. Interesting work
    6. Personal loyalty of supervisor
    7. Tactful discipline
    8. Full appreciation of work done
    9. Help on personal problems
  10. Feeling of being in on things

However, when employees are given the same exercise and asked what affects their morale the most, their answers tend to follow this pattern (mark in the "Employees" column).

    1. Full appreciation of work done
    2. Feeling of being in on things
    3. Help on personal problems
    4. Job security
    5. High wages
    6. Interesting work
    7. Promotion in the company
    8. Personal loyalty of supervisor
    9. Good working conditions
  10. Tactful discipline

Note that the top three items marked by the employees are the last three felt to be important for them by their supervisors.

Discussion Questions:

1. In comparing your group's ratings with that of other employees ("Employees" column), what factors might account for differences of opinion?
2. What might be a reason for supervisory evaluations ("Supervisors" column) being so different from those of their employees ("Employees" column)?
3. If this form were to be used in your department (office, etc.), how similar would the results be?

Materials Required:

Sufficient copies of the form found on the following page.

Approximate Time Required:

20 minutes

Source:

Unknown

WHAT DO PEOPLE WANT FROM THEIR JOBS?

Individual	Group	Factors	Supervisors	Employees
		High Wages		
		Job Security		
		Promotion in the Company		
		Good Working Conditions		
		Interesting Work		
		Personal Loyalty of Supervisor		
		Tactful Discipline		
		Full Appreciation of Work Done		
		Help on Personal Problems		
		Feeling of Being in on Things		

VI
SELF-CONCEPT

Accentuate the Positive

Objective:

To break down self-imposed barriers that don't allow people to "like themselves"; to enhance one's self-image by sharing comments and personal qualities.

Procedure:

Most of us have been brought up to believe that it is not "right" to say nice things about one's self or, for that matter, about others. This exercise attempts to change that attitude by having teams of two persons each share some personal qualities with one another. In this exercise, each person provides his or her partner with the response to one, two, or all three of the following suggested dimensions.

1. Two physical attributes I like in myself
2. Two personality qualities I like in myself
3. One talent or skill I like in myself

Explain that each comment must be a positive one. No negative comments are allowed! (Since most people will not have experienced such a positive encounter, it may take some gentle nudging on your part to get them started.)

Discussion Questions:

1. How many of you, on hearing the assignment, smiled slightly, looked at your partner, and said, "You go first"?
2. Did you find this to be a difficult assignment to start on?
3. How do you feel about it now?

Materials Required:

None

Approximate Time Required:

10 minutes

Source:

Dr. Robert Lindberg, University of Texas at San Antonio

Positive Self-Concept

Objective:

To demonstrate that it _is_ acceptable to verbalize one's own positive qualities.

Procedure:

Have the audience divide themselves into groups of two. Each person is then asked to write on a sheet of paper 4 or 5 things they really like about themselves. (Note: Since most people tend to be overly modest and hesitant to write something nice about themselves, some light encouragement on the facilitator's part may be needed. For example, the trainer may "spontaneously" disclose his or her list, such as "enthusiastic, honest, serious, intelligent, graceful.")

After 3-4 minutes have passed, ask each person to share with their respective partners the items they wrote down.

Discussion Questions:

    1. Did you feel uncomfortable with this activity? If so, why? (We've been culturally conditioned to not expose our egos to others, even if it is valid to do so.)
    2. Were you honest with yourself, i.e., did you "hold back" on your traits?
    3. What reaction did you get from your partner when you disclosed your strengths? (e.g., surprise, encouragement, reinforcement)

Materials Required:

None

Approximate Time Required:

15 minutes

Source:

Unknown

Providing Positive Feedback

Objective:

To encourage people to verbalize positive feelings toward others.

Procedure:

Note: This exercise may be used to follow up the one on Positive
Self-Concept. Divide the group into dyads. Each person is asked
to write 4-5 things they've noticed in their partner. The items
must all be positive ones (neat dresser, pleasant voice, good lis-
tener, etc.). After a few minutes of writing, open discussion
follows for each group of two, wherein the observer states what he
or she wrote about the other.

Discussion Questions:

   1. Were you comfortable with this exercise? If not, why?
(It may be a new experience to be both giver and receiver of positive feedback.)
   2. What would make it easier for us to give positive feedback
to others? (Develop a close relationship first; provide validating
evidence; choose an appropriate time)
   3. What would make it easier for us to receive positive feedback from others? (Practice accepting it with grace; resolve to
ponder its validity first before challenging it; allow yourself to
feel good about it)

Materials Required:

None

Approximate Time Required:

15 minutes

Source:

Unknown

Time to Share

Objective:

To let individuals give positive strokes to others. To subtly force participants to vocally share positive qualities with others.

Procedure:

This activity can be used alone or can follow the exercise, "Accentuate the Positive." (It is best used where participants have previously had the opportunity to share and interact with each other.) After pairing off the group in teams of two, introduce the session by suggesting we all need and crave recognition and positive strokes.

Have each person tell his or her partner the following:

1. One physical feature that is particularly nice
2. One or two personality traits that are unusually pleasant
3. One or two talents or skills that are noteworthy

Suggest that each person record their partner's feelings, thoughts, and feedback and save them to read on a "bummer day."

Discussion Questions:

1. Why is it difficult for many of us to give another person a compliment?
2. Why is it that most people are quick to give a negative comment, but seldom, if ever, have anything nice to say about people?
3. "People tend to behave as we tend to think they should behave." Do you agree or disagree? Why?

Materials Required:

None

Approximate Time Required:

15 minutes

Source:

Dr. Robert Lindberg, University of Texas at San Antonio

VII
LEARNING

Patterns of Learning

Objective:

To illustrate that there are multiple and interrelated methods by which people learn.

Procedure:

Distribute to each trainee a copy of the Kolb Learning Style Inventory (see Kolb et al., Organizational Psychology, 3rd edition, Prentice-Hall, 1979, Chapter 2). Have the participants compute their personal scores on each of the four scales: Concrete Experience, Reflective Observation, Abstract Conceptualization, and Active Experimentation. Obtain from the group a sampling of either the range of scores within each of the scales, or a sampling of the set of scores from several participants. In either approach, it is likely that the data can be used to provide evidence that there is significant variability among individuals in the way in which they learn (assuming the inventory is valid). Then the trainer may proceed to explain the sequential relationship among the four learning styles, and the ways in which the present training program will accent one or more of them. The implications for those persons with low scale scores should then be discussed.

Alternative Procedure:

The trainer could simply begin by explaining the four learning styles (or any other similar paradigm for learning) and ask the trainees to assess themselves on their perceived experience and capacity to use each approach (see following page). Although the data gathered will be subjective, the assessment will have more face validity (and therefore personal acceptance) to each participant.

Discussion Questions:

   1. What are your strengths/weaknesses in how you learn? (e.g., with which styles are you most/least comfortable?)
   2. How will your personal learning style affect your capacity to maximize your learning in this program, given the methods we intend to use? How must you adapt?
   3. What role can I play for you to assist your learning process? (e.g., draw in relevant theories, provide role plays and simulations, assign some structured thinking tasks)

Materials Required:

Kolb's Learning Style Inventory (if permission is obtained to reproduce it) or the following page.

<u>Approximate Time Required</u>:

15-30 minutes

<u>Source</u>:

Kathy Ramsey, Southeast Banking Corporation.

Learning Style Self-Assessment

Directions:

Examine the ways in which you characteristically learn new material. Assess the degree to which you feel most comfortable with each of the following methods (10=very comfortable; 1=least comfortable) by circling one number for each method.

A. Concrete Experience
    (Actual involvement in a task by doing it)

    1   2   3   4   5   6   7   8   9   10

B. Reflective Observation
    (Passively observing others in action and then thinking about it)

    1   2   3   4   5   6   7   8   9   10

C. Abstract Conceptualization
    (Creating integrated meaning out of seemingly independent factors; defining concepts and developing models and theories)

    1   2   3   4   5   6   7   8   9   10

D. Active Experimentation

    1   2   3   4   5   6   7   8   9   10

139

Consciousness and Competence

<u>Objective</u>:

To point out to trainers and trainees the importance of considering trainee movement on both the skill and awareness dimensions.

<u>Procedure</u>:

Ask the participants to think of a skill at which they are particularly adept and another in which they have little expertise (e.g., tennis, bridge, public speaking). Now ask the participants if they know whether they are truly good or bad at that behavior. Then point out that they have been asked to appraise themselves on two dimensions, <u>both</u> of which are critical for the effective development of many <u>skills</u> (e.g., classroom instruction).

Display the model found on the following page to the group. The model illustrates the interaction of competence (low to high) and consciousness (low to high). Point out to the group that it may be essential for a trainer to (a) know the entry level of the trainees; (b) assess their awareness of that level; (c) make them cognizant of their relative incompetence (move from quadrant 1 to 2); (d) increase their skills (move from quadrant 2 to 3); and (e) determine the costs and benefits of finally moving them to stage 4, unconscious competence. Here it should be noted that stage 3 may be the "ideal" for many tasks and persons.

<u>Discussion Questions</u>:

　　1.　Is trainee consciousness of equal importance to competence? Why or why not?　(Consider the readiness-to-learn principle)
　　2.　What techniques are available to increase a trainee's consciousness of his or her competence?　(e.g., needs analysis, performance appraisal sessions, performance data or tests)
　　3.　Would it be useful to share this model with a group of trainees so they could understand the dual objectives of the trainer?

<u>Materials Required</u>:

Handout or transparency of the model found on the following page.

<u>Approximate Time Required</u>:

15 minutes

<u>Source</u>:

"Conscious Competence - The Mark of a Competent Instructor," <u>Personnel Journal</u>, July, 1979, pp. 538-9.

RELATING AWARENESS AND COMPETENCE LEVELS

Self-Awareness

Low   High

	Low	High
Low	1 Unconscious Incompetence	2 Conscious Incompetence
High	4 Unconscious Competence	3 Conscious Competence

Competence

The Trainer's Mirror

Objective:

To help trainers see tasks through the eyes of trainees.

Procedure:

Provide each participant with a small mirror and a sheet of paper
with the figure found on the following page on it. Have the participants place the mirror in front of them, positioned so they
may see the figure in it. Assign them the task of tracing between
the parallel lines, starting at the number 1 and continuing on
around the figure without taking their eyes off the mirror.
Measured either in terms of speed or quality (straightness of the
lines), the participants will have difficulty with the task, and
sense the frustration often endured by trainees when everything
appears backward to them.

Alternative:

Have the participants form pairs. Blindfold one person in each
pair. Provide them with a set of tinkertoys (or Legos, etc.) and
a master model of something to construct. Have each pair compete
against all others (or the clock) to see which "trainer" can
orally aid the trainee most effectively.

Discussion Questions:

    1. Why was it difficult to trace the figure?
    2. In what ways do we as trainers often require trainees to
act as though they were forced to work through mirrors?
    3. What can we do to ease the learning tasks of trainees,
given this insight?

Materials Required:

Mirrors and the figure found on the following page.

Approximate Time Required:

15 minutes, plus discussion time.

Source:

Unknown.

145

THE TRAINER'S MIRROR

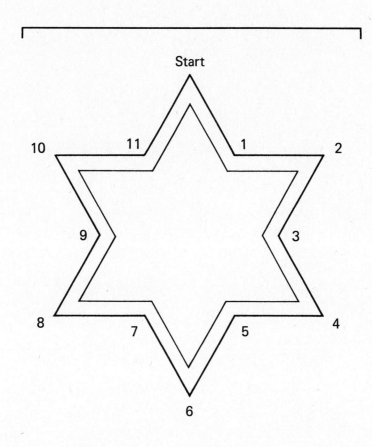

147

The Power of Positive Suggestion

Objective:

To increase the effectiveness of trainee learning by implanting positive expectations in the trainees' minds.

Procedure:

The self-fulfilling prophecy, Pygmalion Effect, and suggestology all present the same basic concept - if people think they are receiving something, they will act in accordance with those expectations. This concept can be used effectively with trainees as well.

For example, the trainer can simply present a set of instructional objectives at the beginning of a session. (An old cliche suggests that "if you tell your trainees what your objectives are, your training problem is 50% resolved.")

A second example is to provide a training group with a set of "testimonials" from past participants. If we hear that other persons we respect have valued the program's content, then we will be more positively oriented toward it.

A third approach is to use discussion groups to respond to the questions of (a) "What do you expect to receive from this session?" or (b) "What comments have you heard from previous participants?" (In this way, they create their own expectations.)

Many other variations are also possible. For example, some trainers will insert a "stooge" into the audience to play a prescribed role as questioner, agitator, or demonstrator of a model for case analysis.

Discussion Questions:

   1. What do you feel about the use of positive suggestion techniques on the job or in training seminars?
   2. What problems may be associated with their use? (e.g., a feeling of being manipulated)
   3. What other applications can you see for this concept?

Materials Required:

None

Approximate Time Required:

5-20 minutes, depending on alternative chosen.

149

150

The Little Boy

<u>Objective</u>:

    1. To stimulate participants to differentiate between education, training, and development.

    2. To point out the ways in which a trainer's best intentions may actually result in constraining trainee activity.

<u>Procedure</u>:

Either read, or distribute copies of the tale of "The Little Boy." (It is a highly poignant story of a little schoolboy who is conditioned by an early classroom environment to void his inherent imagination and creativity. Eventually, it becomes completely stifled. Later, when a new classroom environment provides a new opportunity, he is unable to take advantage of it.) Form small discussion groups (3-5 members). Ask each group to identify and report on the questions of "What implications does this story have for us as trainees/for us as trainers?"

<u>Discussion Questions</u>:

    1. What is the major point of the story?

    2. What is the difference between education, training, and development?

    3. When is it appropriate to engage in each (if they are defined to be different)?

    4. What other illustrations of inappropriate pedagogy can you think of?

<u>Materials Required</u>:

Copies of "The Little Boy" (or it could be read to the group).

<u>Approximate Time Required</u>:

15-20 minutes

<u>Source</u>:

Helen Buckley (Utah Board of Education)

The Number Game

<u>Objective</u>:

To allow participants to discover (or reinforce) some principles of adult learning through "hands-on" activity.

<u>Procedure</u>:

Distribute eight copies of the number game to each participant. Ask them to place a blank sheet of paper over the numbers so they cannot see the placement of the numbers. Tell them this is a simple hand-eye coordination exercise in which they are to work as fast as they possibly can within a given time period. Then tell the participants to "remove the blank sheet of paper. With pen or pencil, draw a line from #1 to #2, #3, etc., until I say 'stop.' OK? Go!"

Allow 60 seconds; then say, "Stop. Please circle the highest number you reached and jot down the number '1' in the upper right hand corner."

Repeat this exact procedure for 6 or 7 more times, each time allowing 60 seconds. Make certain each sheet is numbered in sequence (#1, #2, up to #6 or #7).

<u>Discussion Questions</u>:

    1. In all candor, how did you feel when you were going through the exercise? (Note: Responses will be "nervous," "frustrated," "upset," "mad," etc.)
    2. "Practice makes perfect." If this is really true, we all should have shown a consistent increase in the number attained with each attempt. Is that true for each of you? If not, why?

<u>Materials Required</u>:

A quantity of Number Game sheets (4 per person, printed both sides).

<u>Approximate Time Required</u>:

15 minutes

<u>Source</u>:

Unknown

Learning Curve

<u>Objective:</u>

To plot one's level of learning and to illustrate that "learning plateaus" are commonplace.

<u>Procedure:</u>

Note: This exercise should be used in connection with "The Number Game."

After the participants have completed the seven exercises of the Number Game, have them plot each of the individual results (sequentially) on the learning curve. Interpolate as needed. Connect each of the seven dots to complete your learning curve.

Typical examples of learning curves may be shown to the participants with accelerating learning, decelerating learning, and one with a clear plateau.

<u>Discussion Questions:</u>

    1. Did anyone have an increase every time?
    2. Many of us experienced a slight decline, or "learning plateau." What might cause this?
    3. If our trainees are likely to experience these "plateaus," how can we be more understanding of these situations and adapt to them?

<u>Materials Required:</u>

Learning Curve Sheets (1 per person).

<u>Approximate Time Required:</u>

5-10 minutes

<u>Source:</u>

Unknown

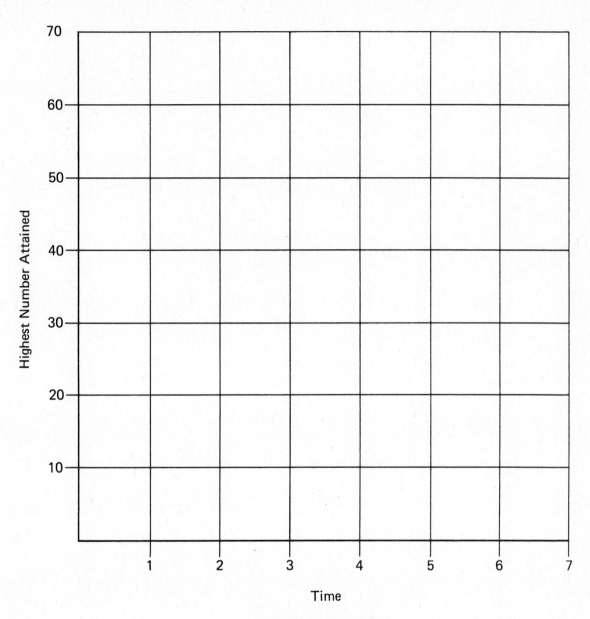

Highest Number Attained

70
60
50
40
30
20
10

1   2   3   4   5   6   7

Time

LEARNING CURVE

159

160

Hand Clasp

<u>Objective</u>:

To demonstrate how forced change may cause discomfort and therefore resistance.

<u>Procedure</u>:

In discussing change and acknowledging that many of us admittedly resist any kind of change, suggest that you would like to illustrate your point. Ask the group to simply clasp their hands with their fingers interlocked in a prayerful fashion.

Tell the group to glance down to see how their thumbs and fingers are interlaced. Now, have them pull their hands apart and reclasp them the exact <u>opposite</u> way (i.e., if one's left thumb were on top initially, the right thumb would now be on top). Point out that for some, this physical change presents no problems, but for most of us, even this slight physical change causes discomfort or simply feels awkward. Therefore, the chances that we will sustain such a behavior are relatively limited.

<u>Discussion Questions</u>;

    1. Did any of you feel uncomfortable with your fingers in the new position? Why?

    2. "People resist change." Do you agree? If so, why?

    3. What are some techniques we can employ to reduce resistance to change?

<u>Materials Required</u>:

None

<u>Approximate Time Required</u>:

5 minutes

<u>Source</u>:

Unknown

162

Arm Folding Exercise

Objective:

To demonstrate one's innate resistance to change - or to being changed.

Procedure:

Ask the group to fold their arms in front of them. Tell them that they should not glance down to identify which arm rests on top of the other. Then ask them to quickly unfold their arms and refold them the opposite way (i.e., if the left arm was initially on top, it should now be underneath the right arm).

Discussion Questions:

    1. Why did you find this awkward? (It was a change from years of old habits)
    2. How does it feel in this new position? (Uncomfortable)
    3. If even this slight physical change may have some built-in resistance, what implications does this have for more substantial physical and intellectual change?

Materials Required:

None

Approximate Time Required:

5 minutes

Source:

Unknown

Recall: Retention of the Brain

Objective:

To vividly illustrate the immediate recall power of the brain; to demonstrate that learned facts can be retrieved almost immediately.

Procedure:

The human brain, with its billions and billions of cells, stores almost every "bit" of knowledge or experience we've encountered. Like a computer, one merely pushes the right "button" to instantly recall items stored from years and years of experience. After expanding or introducing this segment, tell the group you'd like to attempt to demonstrate the aforementioned point of retention and recall. Ask the group to just relax for a moment and then ask, "Who can tell me the name of their first grade teacher?" Past usage of this exercise indicates that at least 3/4's of the group will raise their hands! (An alternative question is to ask the group if they had a dog as a pet when they were youngsters, and what its name was or physical characteristics were.)

Discussion Questions:

    1. When is the last time you thought about your first grade teacher? Why would that name have "popped" into your heads so quickly? (The person was significant; the brain is phenomenal)
    2. Why are some things retained while most items are so quickly forgotten? (We consciously and unconsciously screen in and out various items)
    3. What can you do to more firmly implant ideas, knowledge, etc., in long-term storage? (Repeat them, recall them frequently, associate them with other items)

Materials Required:

None

Approximate Time Required:

5 minutes

Source:

Unknown

Memory Exercise: Learning Numbers

Objective:

To learn a method by which telephone numbers, dates, or any kind of lists of numbers can easily be memorized.

Procedure:

All memory can be improved by basing recall on the law of association. In this case, we will assign the 10 numbers (0-9) a letter(s) which must be first committed to memory.

0 - S, Z	5 - l
1 - T	6 - sh, ch
2 - N	7 - K
3 - M	8 - F
4 - R	9 - P, B

Note that only consonants, not vowels, are used. Assign the letter's value to each number. Now choose a number to be learned, such as the telephone number 9 2 1 - 0 2 4 0. For example, the 921-0240 number is first transferred to P N T - S N R S. Then, through adding vowels any place convenient, try and make a word, phrase, or even a silly set of words. This phone number belongs to a person who happens to drive a Pinto. Using that as a start, the numbers

> 9 2 1 - 0 2 4 0 are filled in as
> PiN To S NoReS

and there is a quick mental image of the friend's car rearing back like a horse and snoring. It is important to get the word picture, "Pinto Snores"! To retrieve the number, simply translate the consonants (not vowels) back to the original numbers.

Note: Before demonstrating this with a group, experiment with several numbers, as it is often time-consuming in the early stages of skill development to be able to insert vowels to make workable word pictures.

Discussion Questions:

1. Do you find it easier to memorize a series of numbers (e.g., phone numbers or padlock combinations) than a single word or phrase? Why or why not?
2. What are some ways in which memory improvement can help you do your job better? (Mentally storing confidential data, memorizing key points for verbal presentations)

<u>Materials Required</u>:

None

<u>Approximate Time Required</u>:

15 minutes

<u>Source</u>:

Several authors on memory development.

Memory Exercise: Key Words

<u>Objective</u>:

To provide a proven vehicle for those called upon to memorize items or long lists of names or things.

<u>Procedure</u>:

Much of what and how we learn is based on association. This exercise will give you a basic list of 10 "key words" you can easily learn and commit to memory. For the sake of simplicity, use your training room or facility (or most any room) to make these associations. Assign each wall and corner a number, starting with the front corner as #1, the wall #2, and so on as shown.

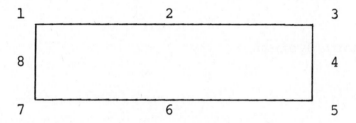

Make the floor #9 and the ceiling #10. Go over and over these designations with the group, i.e., "That wall (point towards it) is number ___," etc., until all 10 numeric designations are memorized. Then start assigning a physical object to each point, as follows:

1 corner - washing machine	6 (wall) - atom bomb
2 (wall) - atom bomb	7 corner - car jack
3 corner - chef	8 (wall) - van
4 (wall) - medicine	9 floor - hair
5 corner - money	10 ceiling - tiles

It is imperative that each assignment be made with an unusual, silly, or even outlandish visual image. For example, "#1 is a huge, 10-foot high <u>washing machine</u> spilling clothes and water all over the place." You must see such an image. Number 2: "Visualize that wall crashing in on us because of an <u>atom bomb</u> explosion," i.e., #2 is "atom bomb." Number 3: "See a 9-foot tall <u>chef</u>, white hat and all, come right through that corner!" Use your imagination to complete the cycle.

After all 10 objects are completely memorized, ask the group who can name all the presidents of the United States. (Doubtless, there will be no takers.) Then ask who knows the first 20. Pause, then ask, "How about the first 10?" Wait momentarily, and then say, "I'll bet we all do." Point to #1 (corner) - the washing machine becomes Washington. #2 (atom bomb) becomes Adams; #3, chef, is Jefferson.

The key word, "medicine," becomes Madison; in #5 (corner), "money" turns to Monroe. Adams, Jackson, Van Buren, Harrison, and Tyler round out the ten.

Tell the participants to "Keep the key words in your memory banks. The next time you want to memorize up to 10 items (key points in a speech, shopping lists, etc.), make up a silly and outlandish association picture with each part of the room! Remember, the sillier the visual imagery, the better recall you will have."

Materials Required:

None

Approximate Time Required:

15 minutes

Source:

Dean Vaugh Memory Systems

Film Recaps

Objective:

To increase the effective integration of films into training programs.

Procedure:

After selecting a film for inclusion in a training program, develop a plan for maximizing its impact on trainee learning and for smoothly integrating the film into the balance of the program. The best model to follow is the classic preacher's adage - "First I tell them what I'm going to tell them, then I tell them, and then I tell them what I told them!" A film recap can be used at either the beginning or end of a film's showing. The recap should be brief (about one page), focus only on the major concepts trainees are expected to retain, and indicate how the film relates to the total program. Used in advance, the recap can be presented in question format, or by the use of a topic outline approach to pique the participants' interest and alert them to what's coming. Used as a follow-up, the recap incorporates the learning principles of repetition, another medium, and reinforcement. (Some film companies provide wallet-size printed highlights of their films, e.g., Ramic Productions.)

Discussion Questions:

    1. (Before distributing the recap) What major points did you feel were presented in the film?
    2. What other points related to the topic were not covered but are seen as important?
    3. In what ways can you see yourself applying the film's concepts?

Materials Required:

Preprinted recap

Approximate Time Required:

5-15 minutes before or after the film.

Source:

Lou Bare, "Using Film Recaps," Training and Development Journal, December, 1978, p. 50.

VIII
COMMUNICATION

"Let's Talk"

Objective:

To break the ice in a group of strangers, or merely to illustrate one's use of gestures and how natural these gestures are to us in verbal communication. This exercise can also demonstrate that verbal communication may become awkward for us when nonverbal gestures or actions are prohibited.

Procedure:

Tell the group that the next few minutes will be devoted to a simple activity wherein they will turn to a person seated nearby and just talk for 2-3 minutes. The subject matter is unimportant; you'd merely like them to converse with someone else (2 to a group) for a few minutes.

After a 2-3 minute period, ask them to stop and tell their partners what they noticed about the other's nonverbal behavior; for example, the person kept fiddling with a pencil, or continually was tapping their fingers, etc. After these gestures have been identified, acknowledge that most of us do these movements almost unknowingly.

After each person has received a "critique" from their partner, tell the group to resume their conversations, but now they must make a conscious effort to use absolutely no nonverbal movements. Have them continue their conversations for 2-3 more minutes.

Discussion Questions:

    1. Were most of us really aware or cognizant of our nonverbal movements in the first conversation?
    2. Did you find any of your partner's gestures distracting or even annoying?
    3. How did it "feel" when we were forced into a strictly verbal discussion? Was the communication as effective without our gestures?

Materials Required:

None

Approximate Time Required:

10-15 minutes

Source:

Unknown

A Nonverbal Introduction

Objectives:

    1. To demonstrate that communication can sometimes be com-
pletely accomplished without words and still be largely effective.
    2. To illustrate that interpersonal communication is indeed
possible through the use of gestures and other nonverbal methods.

Procedure:

Divide the group into two-person teams. State that the purpose of
this exercise is to introduce oneself to his or her partner, but
that this entire activity must be accomplished with no words,
i.e., completely nonverbally. They may use visuals, pictures,
signs, gestures, signals, or anything nonverbal. If necessary,
you may offer certain hints, i.e., pointing to a wedding ring to
indicate marriage, an in-place running movement to indicate
jogging, etc.

After a 2-minute time period allowed for each member of the dyad,
have each group then take a few minutes to verbally "check themselves out," i.e., allow them to verbally state what they were
communicating nonverbally.

Discussion Questions:

    1. How accurate were you in describing yourselves? (Have
them rate themselves on a 1-5 scale.)
    2. How accurate were you in "reading" your partner's ges-
tures? (Rate themselves again)
    3. What were some of the better clues given by your partner?
    4. What barriers or problems seemed to be in our way? (Lack
of props, lack of experience with nonverbal communication)
    5. How might we eliminate or reduce these barriers?

Materials Required:

None

Approximate Time Required:

10 minutes

Source:

Unknown

Hand to Chin Exercise

Objective:

To illustrate that actions may speak louder than words.

Procedure:

As you demonstrate, ask the group to extend their right arms parallel to the floor. State, "Now, make a circle with your thumb and forefinger." (As you speak, demonstrate the action.) Then continue, "Now, very firmly bring your hand to your chin." (<u>Note</u>: As you say, "bring your hand to your chin," bring your hand to your <u>cheek</u>, not to your chin.) Pause. (Most of the group will have done what you have, i.e., brought their hands to their cheeks.) Look around, but say nothing. After 5-10 seconds, a few in the group will realize their error and move their hands to their chins. After a few more seconds, more people will join in the laughter, and your point can then be verbally reinforced--a trainer's actions may speak louder than words.

Discussion Questions:

    1. Did you ever hear the saying, "Don't do as I do; do as I say"? Do we practice this as trainers?
    2. We all know actions speak louder than words. How can we use this knowledge in our jobs to help ensure better understanding?
    3. Communication is always a scapegoat for performance problems. What other barriers to effective communication does this exercise suggest?

Materials Required:

None

Approximate Time Required:

5 minutes

Source:

Unknown

Preconceived Notion

Objective:

To illustrate how a "mind set" can block simple communication.

Procedure:

Before showing the illustration on the following page, simply
state, "Keep the arrow pointing down. If you can read this, please
raise your hand, but don't tell anyone else." As you rotate the
sheet, say, "You don't have to turn it around as I am doing, but
with the arrow pointing downward, can you read what this says?"
(Usually 10-15% of a group will have seen this before or will
detect the word "FLY" quickly.) Acknowledge them immediately, and
ask, "The rest of you can't see the word FLY? If you still can't
see it, try looking at the <u>white</u> space rather than the black
markings."

Discussion Questions:

    1. This type of thing - preconceived notions - is common for
most of us. Can you recall an incident where such notions may
have caused some concerns?
    2. What other barriers cause problems in interpersonal com-
munication? (Noise, disinterested people, wrong methods, etc.)
    3. Children see the word "FLY" immediately. Why, then, do
adults experience difficulty in seeing it as fast? (We have
"learned" to read black print on white paper, such as this page.)

Materials Required:

Sheet like the attached

Approximate Time Required:

5-10 minutes

Source:

Unknown

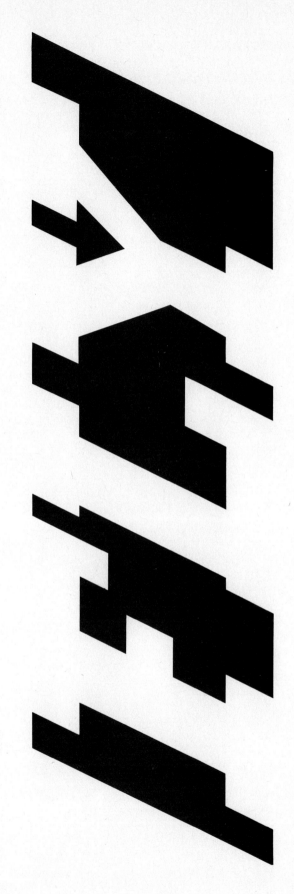

183

The Coat

<u>Objectives:</u>

    1. To demonstrate the danger of assumptions about a trainee's background knowledge and common vocabulary.
    2. To illustrate the advantage of modeling, demonstration, and interaction vs. one-way communication.

<u>Procedure:</u>

Lay a jacket on the table. Select a "volunteer" and inform them that you don't know what the jacket is or what to do with it. The volunteer's task is to train you in the jacket's use as soon as possible. The "trainer" will often engage in telling behaviors whose effectiveness can be distorted by slow learner behaviors by the trainee (e.g., grabbing the pocket when told to grab the collar, or inserting the arm up the sleeve in a reverse direction). The difficulty of completing the assignment can be further exaggerated by depriving the trainer of feedback by having them turn their back to the trainee. After a brief time period of minimal progress, the class can be asked for its assistance. A fruitful alternative, of course, is to <u>show</u> the trainee how to do it. This can effectively illustrate the merits of the classic Job Instruction Training (J.I.T.) approach, which is to:

    1. Explain how to do it
    2. Demonstrate how to do it
    3. Request an explanation of how to do it
    4. Invite the trainee to do it

<u>Alternatives:</u>

The same process can be used with other articles of clothing (e.g., shoes) or even with a box of wooden matches (with the goal of lighting one).

<u>Discussion Questions:</u>

    1. Why did the trainer initially have a difficult time with the task of training? (Because of assumptions about prior knowledge and common vocabulary, because of limited patience for slow learners on a "simple" task, or because of one-way communication)
    2. What are the benefits of demonstration? (Add the sense of sight, and the words take on additional meaning)
    3. What are the benefits of feedback? (Can gauge progress and understanding and satisfaction of trainees)

<u>Materials Required:</u>

A jacket, match box, or other alternative prop.

<u>Approximate Time Required:</u>

15-20 minutes

<u>Source:</u>

R. K. Gaumnitz, University of Minnesota (Minneapolis)

186

One- and Two-Way Communication

Objective:

To demonstrate the many problems of misunderstanding that can occur in a one-way communication.

Procedure:

Prepare a diagram similar to the one shown on the following page. Ask a volunteer to assist in this demonstration. Explain to the audience that the volunteer is going to describe something to them and their task is to simply follow instructions in sketching out the illustration.

Provide the volunteer with the figure shown. Have the volunteer turn his or her back to the audience so no eye contact is possible. The volunteer can use only verbal communication, i.e., no gestures, hand signals, etc. Further, no questions are allowed on the part of the audience. In brief, only one-way communication is allowed. When the exercise is completed, project the correct figure on the overhead projector and ask participants to judge whether their drawings are at all similar to it.

(If time permits, this activity can be immediately followed with another volunteer using a comparable illustration but allowing for full and free two-way communication.)

Discussion Questions:

    1. How many of us got confused and just "quit" listening? Why?
    2. Why was the one-way communication so difficult to follow?
    3. Even two-way communication cannot ensure complete understanding. How can we make our communication efforts more effective?

Materials Required:

Diagram, as shown

Approximate Time Required:

10-20 minutes

Source:

Unknown

ONE WAY COMMUNICATION DIAGRAM

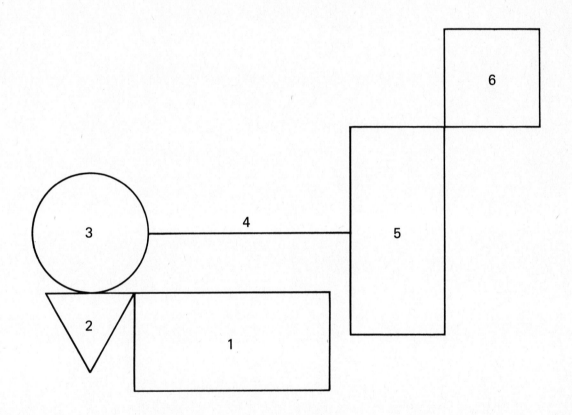

The Aardvark

<u>Objective:</u>

To illustrate that mental imagery or visual aids in communicating or training strongly increase common understanding.

<u>Procedure:</u>

Pass out a sheet or card with the description shown on the following page. Without identifying the object, ask the group to read through this description abstracted from an encyclopedia and then to sketch out or draw whatever kind of picture these printed words give them. (Previous uses produce alligators, pigs, giraffes, elephants, etc. But about a fourth to a third of the group will see this as the aardvark or a close neighbor, the anteater.) After you have announced the correct answer as the aardvark, ask the group to reread the description to see how neatly the words are now reinforced with the mental picture in one's mind.

<u>Discussion Questions:</u>

    1. We know visuals can enhance the learning effort. Why aren't they used more often?
    2. What are some problems inherent in written communication?
    3. Can you recall other incidents where the written word has been the cause of misinterpretation or misunderstandings?

<u>Materials Required:</u>

Cards or paper with the description written on it.

<u>Approximate Time Required:</u>

5-10 minutes

<u>Source:</u>

Unknown

"The body is stout, with arched back;
the limbs are short and stout, armed
with strong, blunt claws; the ears
long; the tail thick at the base and
tapering gradually. The elongated
head is set on a short thick neck,
and at the extremity of the snout is
a disc in which the nostrils open.
The mouth is small and tubular, fur-
nished with a long extensil tongue.
A large individual measured 6 ft.,
8 in. In color it is pale sandy or
yellow, the hair being scanty and
allowing the skin to show."

Reading Exercise

Objective:

To demonstrate that people see what they want to see; to illustrate that even written communication can be misread.

Procedure:

Prepare a card or sheet of paper with the phrases shown on the following page. Hand the sheets out face down and tell the group, "On your sheet (or card), you'll note there are three triangles, each with a brief statement. When I ask you to, turn the sheet over quickly, memorize the three phrases in these triangles, turn your paper back over, and then write, in reverse order, what you have read. OK, proceed." PAUSE for a moment or two and glance at their papers. Continue, "OK, let's check our work...what's the first thing you have written (Note: Most will respond, "Spring the in Paris.")." Even though some will correctly respond with the two articles, i.e., Spring the the in Paris, overlook or ignore them! Ask, "What's the second thing you've written?" Proceed through all three items until the group discovers its error.

Discussion Questions:

1. How could you have interpreted my instructions? (Note: there are several different ways.)

    a. Spring the in Paris; Hand the in Bird; Lifetime in a Once.

    b. Lifetime in a Once; Hand the in Bird; Spring the in Paris.

    c. "In reverse order, what you have read."

2. Why didn't you read the statements correctly? (Familiarity, plus time pressure)
3. Can you see why orders and trainer's instructions to trainees can be misinterpreted?

Materials Required

Sheet or card as shown

Approximate Time Required:

10 minutes

Source:

Unknown

READING EXERCISE

PARIS
IN THE
THE SPRING

BIRD
IN THE
THE HAND

ONCE
IN A
A LIFETIME

Arithmetic Test

<u>Objective:</u>

To demonstrate that people don't always read or follow even simple, written directions.

<u>Procedure:</u>

As shown on the following page, this is a one-page "test." Preface your instructions by commenting that the test is a very simple one involving easy addition, subtraction, multiplication, and division problems. Pass the papers out face down. Then state, "As soon as I say 'Go', turn your papers over and work as <u>fast</u> as you possibly can. As soon as you finish, turn your papers back over, and raise your right hand in the air. Ready - Set - Go!"

Make certain your instructions are given hurriedly and allow no time for questions. Give the impression that time is very tight and they must rush this assignment. Allow only around 30 seconds, and then interrupt, saying, "OK, I see most of you are finished, so let's check our answers." Pause. "The answer to number 1, of course, is what?" (<u>Note</u>: Experience indicates that at least half of the audience <u>will</u> respond.) Acknowledge that "10" is correct, even though one or two people will correctly give the answer as "16."

Continue, "OK, the answer to number 2 is what?" After one or two more responses, demonstrate that there are different answers and ask the group, "Did you all get the same sheet?" Then let the group itself discover their problem by reading the directions to themselves.

<u>Discussion Questions:</u>

    1. Remember the saying, "If all else fails, read the directions"? Why didn't we do so here? (Pressed for time; saw familiar problems)
    2. Have you ever seen incidents where poorly given or rushed instructions may be worse than none at all?
    3. Did anyone experience group pressure when you began to start this exercise? What effects did this have on your performance?

<u>Materials Required:</u>

Test sheet (see following page)

<u>Approximate Time Required:</u> 5-10 minutes

<u>Source:</u> Unknown

Arithmetic Test

In the following simple arithmetic problems, a plus (+) sign means to multiply, a divide (÷) sign means to add, a minus (-) sign means to divide, and a times (x) sign means to subtract. Complete the problems following these directions.

8 + 2 =   14 - 7 =

9 + 11 =   6 x 5 =

4 x 3 =   8 + 3 =

6 ÷ 2 =   7 x 2 =

9 - 3 =   9 + 2 =

7 x 4 =   8 - 4 =

4 + 4 =   9 + 6 =

8 - 4 =   1 ÷ 1 =

12 x 2 =   8 x 7 =

20 - 10 =   13 - 1 =

9 - 1 =   16 - 4 =

5 + 6 =   8 x 2 =

2 x 1 =   9 ÷ 9 =

10 - 5 =   6 x 2 =

12 + 2 =   8 + 4 =

6 ÷ 6 =   10 - 2 =

8 + 5 =   4 - 1 =

6 + 6 =   18 - 3 =

17 x 2 =   8 + 2 =

14 ÷ 7 =   15 x 3 =

IX
LISTENING

Listening and Following Directions

<u>Objectives</u>:

    1. To demonstrate to trainees that the directions given to subordinates may be ambiguous and therefore need greater clarity.
    2. To demonstrate the need to listen carefully and seek clarification of an unclear message.

<u>Procedure</u>:

Show the following page to the group and direct their attention to each quadrant in sequential order. Move rapidly through this set of directions:

    1. <u>Quadrant One</u>: Tell them to place a dot on the letter "i".
    2. <u>Quadrant Two</u>: Tell them to print the word "xerox" in the blank spaces.
    3. <u>Quadrant Three</u>: Tell them you saw a papa bull (PB), a mama bull (MB), and a baby bull (BB) in a barnyard. Which one should not have been there? (Circle one)
    4. <u>Quadrant Four</u>: Tell them to circle the word that doesn't fit with the rest.

The "answers" to these queries are:

    1. <u>Quadrant One</u>: Although most will place a dot in the usual place <u>above</u> the "i", they <u>should</u> have placed it <u>on</u> the "i".
    2. <u>Quadrant Two</u>: Many will write the letters on the lines; however, the directions told them to write it in the blank spaces, e.g., X E R O X.
    3. <u>Quadrant Three</u>: There is, of course, no such thing as a mama bull.
    4. <u>Quadrant Four</u>: The task is to search for the common denominator among three items and exclude the fourth (many will circle the drum). But as one participant said, "You can beat your dog, your child, or a drum, but you just can't beat sex!"

<u>Discussion Questions</u>:

    1. Why did we respond incorrectly? (Ambiguous directions, time pressures, failure to listen, failure to seek clarification, our prior habits and conditioning)
    2. What lessons does this provide us for being better trainers/ trainees/supervisors? (Take action to overcome each of the problems identified in #1)

<u>Materials Required</u>:

Following page on handout card or overhead transparency

206

WORKSHEET FOR FOLLOWING DIRECTIONS

1 ℓ	2 — — — — —
PB MB 3 BB	Drum Dog Sex Child 4

207

Listening Exercise

<u>Objective</u>:

To demonstrate that most adults listen at about a 25% level of efficiency.

<u>Procedure</u>:

Clip a story from a newspaper or magazine that is approximately two or three paragraphs long. With absolutely no introduction, casually mention to your group, "...some of you probably saw the item in the paper the other day," and read aloud the entire two to three paragraphs. When finished, you'll see a room of either bored or disinterested faces. Pull out a dollar bill and state, "OK, I've got a few questions for you based on the story you just heard, and whoever gets them all right wins this dollar." Read eight to ten prepared questions (i.e., names, dates, places, etc.). In all likelihood, not one person will be able to answer <u>all</u> questions correctly.

<u>Discussion Questions</u>:

    1. You all heard that story, yet few could remember very much about it. Why? (Disinterest, no objective, no advance reward)
    2. Why didn't we listen? Is this typical? What can we do to sharpen our listening skills? (See the following page for a list of common suggestions)
    3. If I had told you initially you could win some money, would you have listened more attentively? Why? How can we ensure better listening (without monetary rewards)?

<u>Materials Required</u>:

Any newspaper article with several facts contained therein.

<u>Approximate Time Required</u>:

5-10 minutes

<u>Source</u>:

Unknown

Guides to Good Listening

1. Find an area of interest

2. Judge content, not delivery

3. Delay evaluation

4. Listen for ideas

5. Be flexible

6. Actively work at listening

7. Resist distractions

8. Exercise your mind

9. Keep your mind open

10. Capitalize on thought speed

Following Oral Directions

Objective:

To illustrate the difficulty of attentive listening even in simple exercises.

Procedure:

Ask the group to take a sheet of blank paper and number from 1-15. They are to listen carefully to each question and do all calculations mentally, writing only the answers down on the paper. Read the questions found on the following page at a normal rate of speech.

Discussion Questions:

    1. How many of us just "quit listening" when we got confused or "lost" with a question?

    2. Have you seen times when people seem to "quit listening" when you're giving instructions?

    3. What can we do to prevent this loss of attention or to encourage active listening?

Materials Required:

Questions found on the following page

Approximate Time Required:

5-10 minutes

Source:

Unknown

Worksheet: Following Oral Directions

1. Start with 8; double it; add 4; divide by 5; the answer is ____.

2. Start with 11; subtract 3; add 4; add 3; divide by 3; the answer is ____.

3. Start with 15; add 10; divide by 5; multiply by 6; add 6; divide by 4; the answer is ____.

4. From a number that is 4 larger than 13, add 5; divide by 2; subtract 3; the answer is ____.

5. From a number that is 2 smaller than 9, add 6; add 5; multiply by 2; divide by 4; the answer is ____.

6. Add 6 to 12; subtract 9; add 10; subtract 13; double it; the answer is ____.

7. Add 4 to 5; add 6; add 7; add 9; add 9; divide by 4; the answer is ____.

8. Subtract 6 from 11; add 5; multiply by 5; subtract 15; subtract 10; add 1; the answer is ____.

9. From a number that is 6 larger than 6, add 3; divide by 5; multiply by 4; add 1; the answer is ____.

10. Take the square root of 36; add 5; add 14; divide by 5; add 3; divide by 4; the answer is ____.

11. From a number that is 5 larger than 6, subtract 3; add 2; add 3; add 9; divide by 2; the answer is ____.

12. In the series of numbers, 4-7-8-6-9-12, the first three numbers were _____.

13. In the series of numbers, 4-6-9-9-7-6-3, the sum of the first three numbers is ____.

14. In the series of numbers, 7-9-6-8-4-9-6-10 the lowest odd number is ____.

15. In the series of numbers, 4-5-7-8-6-2-1-9, the sum of these numbers is ____.

Answers:
(1) 4; (2) 5; (3) 9; (4) 8; (5) 9; (6) 12; (7) 10; (8) 26; (9) 13; (10) 2; (11) 11; (12) 4-7-8; (13) 19; (14) 7; (15) 42.

Transmitting Information

<u>Objective:</u>

To demonstrate that information transmitted loses much of its content when passed through "channels."

<u>Procedure:</u>

Take any recent article (2-3 paragraphs) that is not currently "in the news." Divide the group into teams of 4 or 5 people each. Tell them to count off, 1, 2, 3, 4, 5 so that each person is identified in sequence. Ask those numbered as #1 to stay in the room and all others to move outside the room. Then, tell those remaining that you're going to read them a story; they should not take notes, but merely listen to it. After you've read the story (with no questions allowed), ask the #2's to return to their tables, where the #1's will repeat the story to them. Then the #3's are brought in and hear the story from the #2's while the #1's observe. Continue the sequence until all have participated. Then at random have some of the number 5's repeat what they heard.

<u>Discussion Questions:</u>

    1. Of the initial story, how much was lost in the respective transmittals? How much embellishment took place?
    2. What errors or differences were observed as the story passed among the group members?
    3. How could we have increased both the facts and the understanding of the story? How do we get feedback in real world incidents?

<u>Materials Required:</u>

A brief article from a magazine or newspaper

<u>Approximate Time Required:</u>

10-12 minutes

<u>Source:</u>

Unknown

217

Listening Test: Riddles

<u>Objective:</u>

To introduce a session on listening or on communications by showing that few of us really are good listeners. By the use of a humorous, light exercise such as these riddles, the participants are quickly shown that their own skills in listening can be improved.

<u>Procedure:</u>

Ask the group to take a sheet of paper and number from 1-10 on it. Tell them you are going to ask them a series of questions, all of which have short answers. They are to simply jot down their responses on their sheets. Read each question only <u>once</u>.

Now check their answers (see the key below). Ask, "How many said 'Yes' for #1? How many said 'No'?" (A few chuckles will prompt the group that something may be wrong.) Then read the questions again, providing them with the appropriate commentary. Repeat the process for the other nine questions.

<u>Key:</u>

   1.   There's no law against a man's marrying his widow's sister, but it would be the neatest trick of the week. To have a widow, he would have to be dead.
   2.   You'd get one hour's sleep. Alarm clocks don't know the difference between morning and night.
   3. Oh, yes. They have a 4th of July in England. They also have a 5th and a 6th, and so on.
   4.   First of all, you'd light the match.
   5.   Moses took no animals at all. It was Noah who took two of each.
   6.   Who said the Yankees and the Tigers were playing against each other in those games!
   7.   The average man has one birthday; so does the average woman. All the rest are birthday anniversaries. In fact, in France "birthdays" are known as "anniversaires" (anniversaries).
   8.   You can't bury survivors under any law - especially if they still have enough strength to object!
   9.   The archeologist is a liar because B.C., of course, means "Before Christ," and who could have guessed in advance when Christ would be born?
   10.   The bear who rang the doorbell would have to be a white bear. The only place you could build a house with four southern exposures is at the North Pole, where every direction is South.

Discussion Questions:

1. How many did you get right/wrong?
2. Why didn't you get a perfect score?
3. Why is listening called an active process?

Materials Required:

None (or attached sheet)

Approximate Time Required:

10 minutes

Source:

Unknown

Listening Test: Riddles

1. Is there any federal law against a man's marrying his widow's sister?

2. If you went to bed at eight o'clock at night and set the alarm to wake up at nine o'clock in the morning, how many hours of sleep would you get?

3. Do they have a 4th of July in England?

4. If you had only one match and entered a cold room that had a kerosene lamp, an oil heater, and a wood stove, which would you light first for maximum heat?

5. How many animals of each species did Moses take aboard the Ark with him during the great flood?

6. The Yankees and the Tigers play 5 baseball games. They each win 3 games. No ties or disputed games are involved. How come?

7. How many birthdays does the average man have? The average woman?

8. According to International Law, if an airplane should crash on the exact border between two countries, would unidentified survivors be buried in the country they were traveling to, or the country they were traveling from?

9. An archeologist claims he has dug up a coin that is clearly dated 46 B.C. Why is he a liar?

10. A man builds an ordinary house with four sides, except that each side has a southern exposure. A bear comes to the door and rings the doorbell. What color is the bear?

X
PERCEPTION

Mismatched Job Perceptions

Objective:

To catch the audience's attention and encourage them to introspec-
tively analyze their own job situations.

Procedure:

Ask the group to think of the major dimensions of their jobs. Then
ask them to predict how many of those responsibility areas their
boss would list if he or she were asked to do so. Now show the
group the chart found on the following page which portrays the
"typical" 25% lack of overlap between superior-subordinate job
perceptions.

Discussion Questions:

    1. Ask the group to report what they feel would be the pro-
portion of non-overlap in their own job situations.
    2. Ask them why there might be such a disparity.
    3. Ask them how to prevent/resolve such a problem.

Alternative Procedures:

    1. Ask the group to make similar pairs of estimates regarding
(a) the personal qualifications needed to perform their jobs; (b)
the future job changes that are serving to redefine their jobs; and
(c) the obstacles to effective job performance. (Most estimates of
non-overlap will be even higher.)
    2. Ask them to engage in the perceptual process with regard
to their subordinates instead.
    3. Ask them to interview their boss (or subordinates) to deter-
mine the actual areas of non-overlap.

Materials Required:

Attached chart on a transparency or handout.

Approximate Time Required:

10-15 minutes

Source:

William E. Reif, Arizona State University

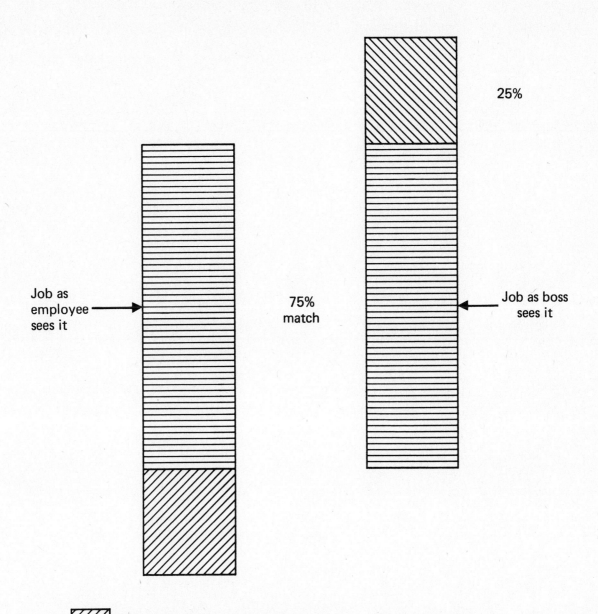

25%

Job as
employee →
sees it

75%
match

Job as boss
sees it

Key:

What the employee is paying attention to that the boss does not
perceive to be important.

What the boss expects the employee to pay attention to, but the
employee does not perceive it as important.

Areas of agreement between boss and subordinate

I'm OK, but Are They?

Objectives:

    1. To demonstrate that people generally tend to evaluate themselves as better than average.
    2. To point out the mathematical impossibility involved if everyone uses the same perceptual set.

Procedure:

Ask group members to rate themselves on a 5-point scale on either a physical, psychological, or behavioral dimension. Examples could be physical attractiveness, interpersonal warmth, or frequency of engaging in ethical behavior. Then ask the group to rate, on another 5-point scale, the typical person (in the group or in society) on the same dimension. Remind the group before each evaluation that the midpoint of the scale is to represent "average."

Collect the data on self-evaluation and compute the mean. Collect the data on evaluation of the "typical" person and calculate the mean.

Discussion Questions:

    1. Which mean do you predict will be higher (quite likely, the self-evaluation will be higher)? Why? (Most people want to view themselves as above average.)
    2. What is the effect of this phenomenon on performance appraisal ratings? On the assessment of the effectiveness of instructors and courses?
    3. What can be done to increase the objectivity of such evaluations? (Use behaviorally anchored scales; use a forced distribution system, or supplement the data with evaluations by outside raters who are less emotionally involved.)

Materials Required:

One prepared question; possibly a printed set of evaluative scales.

Approximate Time Required:

15-20 minutes

Source:

John W. Newstrom and William A. Ruch, "The Ethics of Management and the Management of Ethics, " MSU Business Topics, Winter, 1975, pp. 29-37.

How Observant Are We?

Objective:

To demonstrate that people are often not too observant about
ordinary things.

Procedure:

Ask someone in the group if you may borrow their watch for a moment.
(Caution: Make certain it is a non-digital type.) Tell that person (after the watch's receipt) that you would like to test his or
her powers of observation, and ask the entire group to silently
"play along" with the individual whose watch you are using. Tell
the individual to assume that the watch was lost and you found it.
But, before you return it, you want to make certain the watch can
be identified as being theirs. Some sample questions include,
"What's the brand name?" "What color is the face?" "Anything else
printed on the face?" "Roman or Arabic numerals?" "All 12?"
"Does the watch have the date and/or day on it?" "Second hand?",
etc.

If the group is silently responding as the volunteer attempts to
vocally answer the questions, the point is more easily made (i.e.,
most people cannot totally and accurately describe their own time-
piece even if they look at it dozens of times a day).

Discussion Questions:

    1. Besides me, who else flunked this test? Why?
    2. Why aren't we more observant? (time pressure, lack of
concern, taking things for granted, etc.)
    3. Have you seen incidents where people have overlooked
commonplace things and problems may have resulted?

Materials Required:

A non-digital watch

Approximate Time Required:

5 minutes

Source:

Unknown

Count the F's

Objective:

To illustrate that people see what they want to see; items of prominence catch our attention while seemingly less important items may pass on by.

Procedure:

Pass out face-down copies of the following page to the group. When everyone is ready, ask them to turn the paper over and simply count how many times the letter "f" appears on their sheet. Allow only a minute, and then ask, "How many of you have the sheet with the 3 F's?" (Roughly half the group can be expected to so indicate.) "Who has 4 F's on their sheet?...How about 5?...Does anyone have 6?" (About 50% of the group will see only 3 F's, and approximately 10% will see all 6 F's. The rest see either 4 or 5 on the sheet.)

Alternative:

Ask those with 4, 5, or 6 F's on their sheets to raise their hands and let those with 3 F's exchange papers so they too can "see" all 6 F's. Most will still have a difficult time identifying all 6 of the F's.

Discussion Questions:

1. Why couldn't all of us initially see all 6 F's? (The F in the word "of" sounds like a "V".)
2. Have you observed situations where only the important things get attention? Who decides what's important?
3. How can we persuade people to pay more attention to detail? Is it always important?

Materials Required:

Card or sheet of paper as shown.

Approximate Time Required:

5-10 minutes

Source:

Unknown

COUNT THE F'S

FEATURE FILMS ARE THE RE-
SULT OF YEARS OF SCIENTI-
FIC STUDY COMBINED WITH
THE EXPERIENCE OF YEARS

The Misplaced Dot

Objective:

To be able to judge an object (person) in terms of its relevant dimensions, while screening out the irrelevant dimensions.

Key:

To avoid being visually influenced by the converging lines at the apex of the triangle.

Procedure:

Display the triangle found on the following page to the participants via handout or visual aid. Ask them to assess whether the dot is:

    a. Closer to the top than the base of the triangle
    b. Closer to the base than the top of the triangle
    c. Midway between the top and the base (the correct answer)

Alternatives:

Provide a blank triangle; direct the participants to place a dot midway between the top and bottom. Then either display a correctly placed dot and measure the participants' accuracy by the overlay of a triangle with a vertical scale marked in deviations of 10% from the correct dot, or ask the participants to physically measure (with a ruler) the actual distance from the dot to the top and bottom.

Discussion Questions:

    1. Why were you relatively accurate (inaccurate) in this task?
    2. What are some illustrations of real-life constraints that affect your perception of events?
    3. How can we overcome (prevent) such forces?

Materials Required:

Handout or transparency with the figure found on the following page.

Approximate Time Required:

5 minutes, plus discussion

Source:

Games, September/October, 1978, p. 14.

KEY: THE MISPLACED DOT

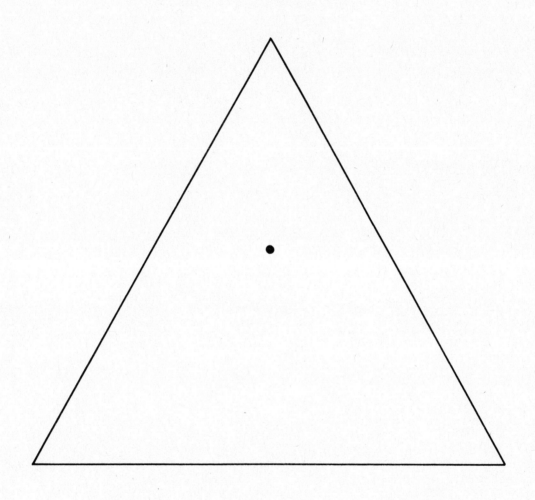

The Lemon Exchange

Objective:

To vividly illustrate the importance of individual differences, the need for astute observational skills, and sensitivity to personal characteristics.

Procedure:

Bring an adequate supply of lemons (or almost any fruit).

   1.   Distribute one to each member of the group. Direct each person to examine their lemon carefully by rolling it, squeezing it, fondling it, inspecting it, etc. Ask them to get to know their lemon (always good for a few laughs). Tell them to pick a name for it. Encourage them to identify in their minds the strengths and weaknesses of their lemon.
   2.   Collect all the lemons and visibly mix them up in front of the group.
   3.   Spread out all the lemons on a table, and ask all persons to come forward and select their original lemon. If conflicts develop over their choices, assist the parties in reconciling their differences, or simply note the failure to agree and use that as a basis for later discussion. (Note: In smaller groups of up to 25 persons, the vast majority successfully identify their own lemon.)

Discussion Questions:

   1.   How many are very sure they reclaimed their original lemon? How do you know?
   2.   What parallels are there between differentiating many lemons and differentiating many people? What differences are there?
   3.   Why can't we get to know people just as rapidly as we did our lemons? What role does the skin play (for lemons and for people)?
   4.   What action principles of human behavior does this bring to light?

Materials Required:

A sufficient quantity of lemons (or other appropriate substitute)

Approximate Time Required:

20-30 minutes

Source: Unknown

Old Woman/Young Woman

Objective:

To illustrate the impact of a person's background or attitudes on their perception of an object or event.

Procedure:

Show the group the illustration found on the following page, and tell them it is a picture of (a) a relatively unattractive, poorly dressed elderly woman, or (b) an attractive, wealthy young woman with a fancy hairdo. Based upon direction (a) or (b), ask how many of them clearly recognize the old/young woman. Then proceed to reverse the directions with the same picture for the benefit of those who see the "other" person, explaining that (with apologies) you really brought the other picture instead. Again inquire how many see the old/young woman.

Alternatives:

Divide the group into two halves. Show the picture to one half, explaining it to be the old woman. Show a duplicate picture to the other half, explaining it to be the young woman. Ask how many in each group recognize the assigned image. Then reverse the pictures and reverse the questions for each group.

Discussion Questions:

    1. How does our mental set (attitude) influence our perception?
    2. What other common attitudes do we have that influence daily activities?
    3. What can be done to open up our minds (as trainees) to new learning?

Materials Required:

Either a picture large enough to be seen throughout the group, or a transparency.

Approximate Time Required:

5-10 minutes, plus discussion

Source:

Edwin G. Boring, "A New Ambiguous Figure," American Journal of Psychology, July, 1930, p. 444. (Originally drawn by cartoonist W. E. Hill, published in Puck, November 6, 1915.)

245

Mind over Matter

<u>Objective:</u>

To demonstrate that the power of the mind is such that mental suggestions can actually cause physical movement.

<u>Procedure:</u>

Ask the group to clasp their hands together with the two fore-fingers extended parallel at a distance of 1-2", as illustrated below.

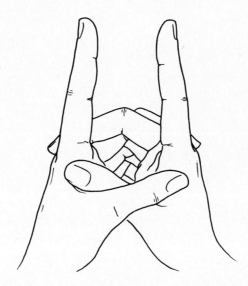

Tell them to study their forefingers and imagine there is a tight rubber band around them. Now state in a deliberate tone and in a slow speed, "You can feel that rubber band bringing your fingers closer...and closer...and closer..." The smiles and laughter of at least half your audience will tell you they are getting the message, and their fingers are closing together. Experience indicates that half to two-thirds of a group will respond accordingly.

<u>Discussion Questions:</u>

    1. What prompted your fingers to move?
    2. Have you observed other incidents where mental suggestions have prompted action?
    3. For those whose fingers remained motionless, what were you doing to counteract the "rubber band"?

<u>Materials Required:</u> None

<u>Approximate Time Required:</u>

5 minutes

<u>Source:</u>

Unknown

XI
PROBLEM SOLVING
AND CREATIVITY

Golf Ball in the Bag

Objective:

To stimulate participants to learn new ways of thinking.

Key:

Taking a reverse perspective from the ordinary (standing the problem on its head).

Procedure:

Relate the following incident to the participants:

> It was the 16th hole in the annual Bob Hope Desert
> Classic, and the tall, handsome newcomer had an
> excellent chance of winning. His iron shot fell just
> short of the green, giving him a good chance for a
> birdie. Smiling broadly, he strode down the fairway
> only to stop in dismay. His ball had rolled into a
> small paper bag carelessly tossed on the ground by
> someone in the gallery.
>
> If he removed the ball from the bag, it would cost
> him a penalty stroke. If he tried to hit the ball
> and the bag, he would lose control over the shot.
> What should he do?

Discussion Questions:

1. What are the ways in which we would try to solve the problem?
2. What is the common element in our approaches? (Ask them to state the problem. It will probably be to "get the ball out of the bag.")
3. What is an alternative way to state the problem (get the bag away from the ball)? Disclose the answer (set fire to the bag).
4. What are some areas in which such a principle (reversing the typical approach) could help us solve problems?

Materials Required:

None, although a golf ball, paper sack, and matches would add realism to the illustration.

Approximate Time Required:

10 minutes

Source:

Eugene Randsepp, "Are You a Creative Executive?", Management
Review, February, 1978, pp. 10-15.

A Piece of Cake

Objective:

To approach a problem from different perspectives.

Key:

To listen carefully to precise wording of a task (or to envision a 2-dimensional object as being 3-dimensional).

Procedure:

Display a large circle to the participants. Ask them to individually divide it into as many pieces as they can by making 4 straight cuts with a long knife. The correct answer is 11, as shown below.

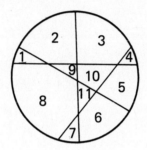

Alternatives:

Describe the object as a cake (3-dimensions implied). The correct answer is then 14, as shown below, with the fourth cut being horizontally through the cake.

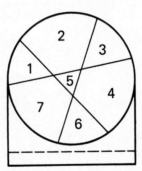

Discussion Questions:

1. How does the statement of a problem affect the trainee's approach to solving it?
2. What are some guidelines to more effective problem (task) statements?
3. How does this relate to the way we make assignments to subordinates, or give direction to trainees?

<u>Materials Required:</u>

Transparencies or flipcharts with (a) the blank circle; (b) wrong
solutions (8, 9, or 10 pieces); and (c) the correct solution shown.

<u>Approximate Time Required:</u>

5 minutes, plus discussion.

<u>Source:</u>

Unknown

The "IX" Exercise

Objective:

To illustrate that problem-solving may not be as difficult as it initially may seem.

Procedure:

Draw the symbol "IX" on a chalkboard or flipchart (or use the figure found on the following page). Ask the group members to make a 6 (six) out of the symbol with the use of only one line.

The correct answer is SIX.

Most people will assume the answer would be more difficult and are surprised to see such a simple solution. Further, most in the audience will assume the answer would have to do with the Roman numeral IX (9) and therefore will find it difficult to see another kind of solution.

Discussion Questions:

1. How many interpreted the IX to be the Roman numeral for "9"?
2. What is the impact of our assumption about the nature of a problem?
3. What lessons for problem-solving and creativity can we draw from this exercise?

Materials Required:

Chalkboard, flipchart, or handout using the figure on the following page.

Approximate Time Required:

5 minutes

Source:

Unknown

IX EXERCISE

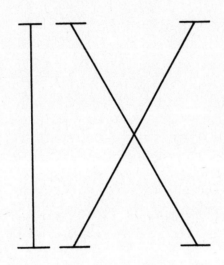

258

The Unseen Square

Objective:

To break out of traditional ways of thinking.

Key:

Using angles instead of squares.

Procedure:

Provide each participant (or group of 3-5 persons) with a pre-cut figure of the external dimension (proportion) shown below. Assign them the task of creating a single square by making only two straight cuts and reassembling the pieces so that all material is used in the final product.

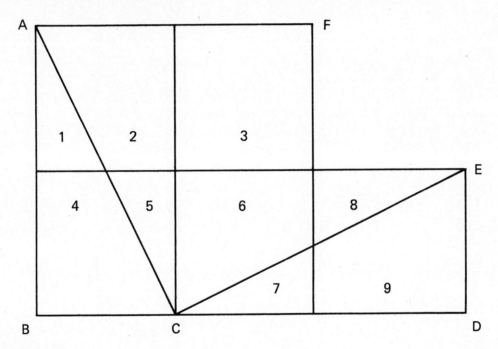

Alternative:

Include the interior vertical and horizontal lines, which simultaneously help and hinder the participants.

Discussion Questions:

    1. What factors in the situation or your experience <u>hindered</u> your progress in solving the task?

    2. What factors in the situation or your experience <u>helped</u> your progress in solving the task?

3. What did you learn that can now be applied to your job/life?

4. What specific applications does that learning have?

Materials Required:

Design traced onto stiff paper; scissors; master "key" for demonstration of correct result (see following page).

Approximate Time Required:

15 minutes

Source:

Unknown

KEY: THE UNSEEN SQUARE

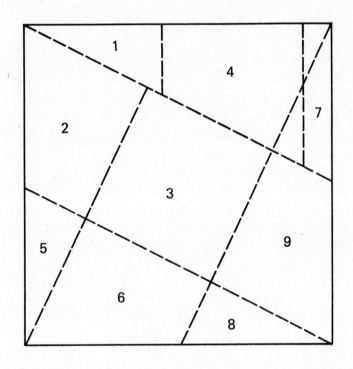

The Farmer's Land Bequest

Objective:

To encourage creative thought.

Key:

Stratifying (partitioning) a larger problem into smaller pieces and rearranging a mental set into a different view.

Procedure:

Provide each participant with a handout illustrating the shape of a piece of land (see following page). Explain the task: To subdivide a farmer's property upon his death into four pieces of equal size and shape for distribution to his four offspring. All land given to each offspring must be adjoining itself (e.g., it cannot be distributed piecemeal). The following is the key.

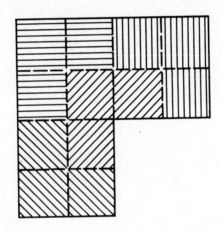

Discussion Questions:

    1. What previous experiences have you had that made it more difficult/easier for you to solve this problem?
    2. What general problem type is this? What other problems are like this?
    3. What general principle(s) could you invoke to aid you in solving future problems of a similar nature?

Materials Required:

Design found on the following page; master key available for distribution via chalkboard, overhead, flipchart, or handout.

<u>Approximate Time Required:</u>

15-20 minutes

<u>Source:</u>

Adapted from N. R. F. Maier, <u>Problem</u> <u>Solving</u> <u>and</u> <u>Creativity</u> <u>in</u>
<u>Individuals</u> <u>and</u> <u>Groups</u> (Belmont, CA: Brooks/Cole, 1970), pp. 96-7.

THE FARMER'S LAND

A Person Bought a House

Objective:

To get trainees to factor a problem into its proper components and relationships.

Key:

Trainees must develop a rational arithmetic system for tracing the profit/loss. It can be done by adding the two proceeds and subtracting the two investments. The danger is to use some of the numbers more than once.

Procedure:

Participants are provided with a written description of the following incident.

> "A person bought a house for $60,000. Soon thereafter, they sold it for $70,000, upon moving out of town. A few months later, they were transferred back to town and purchased the same house for $80,000. Then the person grew tired of the house and resold it for $90,000."

> Question: How much money did the person gain/lose (or break even) on the exchange?

First ask the participants to solve the problem individually. Then join them into small groups of 3-5 persons to resolve the problem on a collective basis (reaching total consensus). Then poll the group to determine the frequency with which each of the following answers was obtained.

> Gained $20,000
> Gained $10,000
> Broke even
> Lost $10,000
> Lost $20,000

Discussion Questions:

1. What factors prevent us from solving the problem correctly?
2. Why were the groups able to solve the problem with greater accuracy?
3. What lessons does this hold for similar problems?

Materials Required:

A preprinted description of the incident.

<u>Approximate Time Required:</u>

15-30 minutes

<u>Source:</u>

Adapted from N. R. F. Maier and A. R. Solem, "The Contribution of
a Discussion Leader to the Quality of Group Thinking: The
Effective Use of Minority Opinions," <u>Human</u> <u>Relations</u>, 1952, 5,
pp. 277-288.

The Nine Dots

Objective:

To suggest to trainees that their pre-existing mental set might constrain their capacity to learn new ideas.

Key:

To force one's mind to expand beyond the self-imposed "box" created by the nine dots.

Procedure:

Display to the group the following configuration of nine dots. Ask them to reproduce the dots on a sheet of their own paper. Assign them the task of connecting all nine dots by drawing four straight continuous lines (without lifting their pencils or retracing a line). Allow them a few minutes to make several attempts. Ask how many solved the task successfully. Then either ask a volunteer to step forward and display the correct solution, or else show them the key (found on the following page) on an overhead transparency projector.

```
   .        .        .


   .        .        .



   .        .        .
```

Alternative Solutions:

1. The task can also be solved with three straight continuous lines. The first starts at the top of the upper left dot, extends through the center of the upper middle dot, on through the bottom of the upper right dot, and out beyond that dot. The second line returns through the second set of three dots, descending gradually from right to left. The last line returns through the bottom three dots.
2. Another approach is to fold the paper so the three lines of dots align closely. Then a single (wide) pencil line will touch all nine dots simultaneously.
3. A third approach is to take a paint brush and, with a single sweep, connect all nine dots simultaneously.

Discussion Questions:

   1. What is the impact in our minds of the configuration of
the nine dots? (We mentally create a square and try to circum-
scribe it with the four lines, leaving the center dot untouched.)
   2. What is the key to solving the puzzle? (Get out of the
boxes that we, or others, create for ourselves.)
   3. What implications does this exercise have for our training program and for our jobs?

Materials Required:

A means of displaying the nine dots and the solution.

Approximate Time Required:

5-10 minutes

Source:

Unknown

KEY: THE NINE DOTS

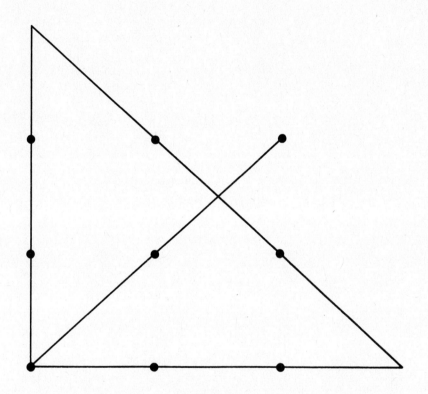

The Sixteen Dots

<u>Objective</u>:

To allow trainees the chance to apply the principle learned in "The Nine Dots" exercise.

<u>Key</u>:

To force one's mind to expand beyond the self-imposed "box" created by the sixteen dots.

<u>Procedure</u>:

Display to the group the following configuration of sixteen dots. Ask them to reproduce the dots on a sheet of their own paper.

```
    .        .        .        .


    .        .        .        .


    .        .        .        .


    .        .        .        .
```

Assign them the task of connecting all sixteen dots by drawing six straight continuous lines (without lifting their pencils or retracing a line). Allow them a few minutes to make several attempts. Ask how many solved the task successfully. Then either ask a volunteer to step forward and display the correct solution, or else show them the key on the overhead transparency projector (see following page).

<u>Alternative Solutions</u>:

The task can be solved with four straight lines, or as few as one (see nine-dot alternative solutions).

<u>Discussion Questions</u>:

    1. What is the key to solving the exercise?
    2. Did the principle learned in the nine-dot exercise help solve this one?
    3. What implications does this exercise have for this training program and for our jobs?

<u>Materials Required:</u>

A means of displaying the sixteen dots, and the solution.

<u>Approximate Time Required:</u>

5-10 minutes

<u>Source:</u>

Unknown

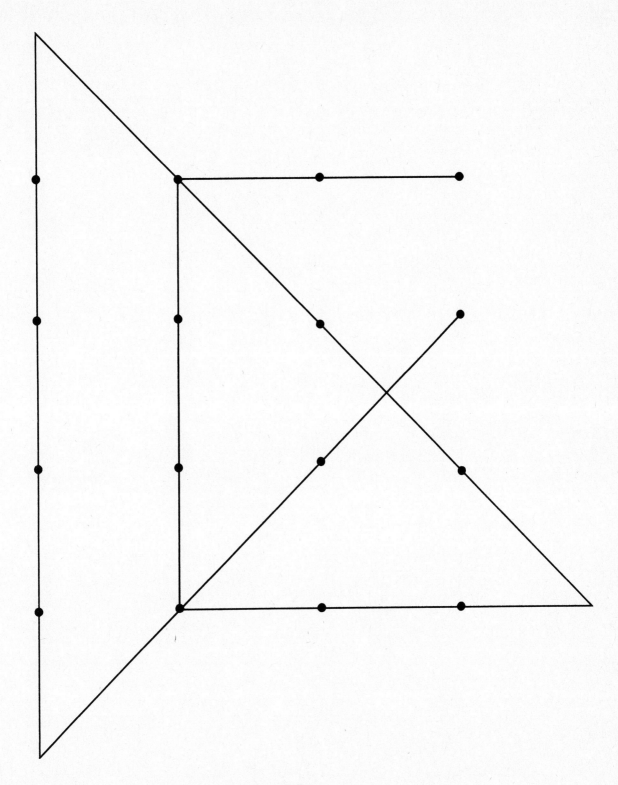

275

Hidden Squares

Objective:

To encourage participants to dig deeper into problems, and visualize them from a different perspective; to see not only the whole, but also various combinations of parts.

Procedure:

Participants are provided with a visual drawing of a large square, divided as shown below. They are then directed to quickly count the total number of squares seen, and report that number orally.

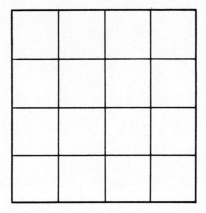

Key:

The correct answer is 30, developed as follows: 1 whole square, 16 individual squares, 9 squares of 4 units each, and 4 squares of 9 units each.

Discussion Questions:

    1. What factors prevent us from easily obtaining the correct answer? (We stop at the first answer, we work too fast)
    2. How is this task like other problems we often face? (Many parts comprise the whole)
    3. What can we learn from this illustration that can be applied to other problems?

Materials Required:

A flipchart, transparency, or handout with the figure found on the following page.

<u>Approximate Time Required</u>:

5 minutes

<u>Source</u>:

Unknown

HIDDEN SQUARES FIGURE

XII
EVALUATION

Pretesting Trainees

Objective:

Various, as listed below.

Procedure:

Pretests have multiple potential uses. They can be used to determine who does and does not need training, which content areas need more and less time, provide a baseline of knowledge or skill to compare post-test scores against, corroborate the needs analysis results, or simply alert trainees to the major topics to be covered. Naturally, the format chosen, depth of material covered, and even anonymity allowed will vary greatly depending on the primary objective to be served.

For illustrative purposes, the technique displayed effectively by Don Kirkpatrick in his national presentations on "Evaluation of Training" will be described. At the beginning of a session, trainees are asked to take a sheet of paper, sign their names, and number from 1-10. (The typical questions are shown on the following page.)

Scoring the test follows immediately. Humor can be injected (e.g., 50 points for signing their names correctly). Group results can be obtained by a quick show of hands and tabulation on a flipchart, or individual papers can be collected. The presentation of the item answers allows the trainer to preview the session material, as well as set the tone for the session. Finally, the collection of pretest data allows the trainer to weave into the later presentation several useful related points (e.g., how a pretest sensitizes a group to a post-test).

Discussion Questions:

1. What are the pros and cons of pretests?
2. How could pretests be used productively by supervisors and other administrators?

Materials Required:

Advance preparation of questions

Approximate Time Required:

15 minutes (without discussion)

Source: Donald Kirkpatrick, University of Wisconsin (Extension)

Pretesting Trainees

"Pretest" on Evaluation

1-4. What are the four criteria commonly used in evaluating training programs?
(Reaction, Learning, Behavior, Results)

5. Which criterion is most frequently used? (Reaction)

6. What is a group that receives training called?
(Experimental)

7. What is a group that does not receive training called?
(Control)

8. What is an evaluation of a group before they receive training called? (Pretest)

9. What is an evaluation after a group receives training called? (Post-test)

10. True or False. The classroom trainer is the person in the best position to evaluate the training program.
(False)

Instant Evaluation Forms

Objectives:

    1. To review and reinforce the learning from the day's session for the trainer.
    2. To provide the trainer with early feedback on the progress made each day.

Procedure:

Design a brief and straight-forward evaluation form that allows for easy accumulation of trainee reactions to the day's session. The form might, for example, focus on three elements:

    1. How valuable was today's session for you? (5-point scale)
    2. What are the most important things you learned today?
    3. How do you intend to apply those ideas to your job?

Distribute and collect the (anonymous) forms during the last 10 minutes of each day's session. Tabulate the responses and prepare a brief analysis of the information gained, and share the analysis with the group at the beginning of the next day's session. Use the presentation as a basis for a concise review, clarification of mis-perceptions, and as a foundation for introducing the new day's topics.

Discussion Questions and Important Points:

    1. What techniques or methods used in yesterday's session contributed most to your learning experience?
    2. How did the group's consensus of important points learned match your own? Why was there a difference?
    3. What are the forces that will encourage (and discourage) you from applying the best ideas back on the job?

Materials Required:

Predesigned reaction sheet

Approximate Time Required:

10 minutes at the end of the session, 20-30 minutes between sessions, and 10-20 minutes at the beginning of the next session.

Source:

Thomas J. Murtha, "Make Your Course Evaluation Work," Training & Development Journal, July, 1979, pp. 50-51.

Grade Your Partner

Objective:

To sensitize part-time or new trainers to the experience of evaluating and being evaluated by others, based on criteria which are
largely unknown.

Procedure:

Provide everyone with a slip of paper. Ask each person to observe
their partner (i.e., the person on their left) briefly and grade
them on a scale from 0-100%. Then have them pass the paper to the
graded person. The trainer may call for a quick report to determine the frequency distribution and range of reported "grades."

Discussion Questions:

    1. What feelings did you have when you were asked to grade
someone else on this basis? (e.g., confused, lost, uptight,
skeptical)
    2. How did you feel when you knew you were going to be
graded? (e.g., concerned, tense, confident, anticipatory, fearful)
    3. What was your first thought when you received your grade?
(e.g., relieved, angry, proud, curious)

Materials Required:

None

Approximate Time Required:

15 minutes

Source:

Unknown

XIII
TRANSFER OF TRAINING

Letter to the Trainer

Objectives:

    1. To facilitate transfer of training to the job.
    2. To feed back information on the concepts found to be most useful on the job.

Procedure:

Prepare a blank letter, survey form, or periodic journal format similar to the one found on the following page. The letter format can be distributed at the end of a program with a specific due date (e.g., in thirty days). It is unstructured. The danger is the low response rate that is likely unless a follow-up is used, or participants are highly committed. The survey format permits the use of greater structure to the responses, and is more likely to obtain a respectable response rate and meaningful data if it is kept brief. The journal approach requires considerable persistence on the part of the participant. However, if rigorously followed, the journal may contain some of the most useful spontaneous insights. The main point, of course, is that the trainees, having been alerted to the certainty of some follow-up mechanism, will be more likely to retain their newly-acquired knowledge and practice their new skills.

Discussion Questions:

Since this is a post-training device, in-training discussion is less relevant. However, discussion similar to the structure proposed in "Letter to My Boss" and "Letter to Myself" would be equally appropriate.

Materials Required:

Letter, survey, or journal format.

Approximate Time Required:

None during the training session.

Source:

Charles M. Vance, "Personal Journals in Training," Training and Development Journal, August, 1979, pp. 54-5.

Letter to the Trainer

Dear _____:

I attended the _____course conducted
by you on _____, 19___. I wish to share with
you a series of insights I have gained since then regarding the
ways in which I have (have not) been able to apply the material to
my job.

I have done the following:

1.

2.

3.

Information in these areas has proven to be of considerably less
use to me:

1.

2.

3.

The suggestions I have for you include:

1.

2.

3.

Signed_____

Letter to My Boss

<u>Objective</u>:

To facilitate transfer of training to the job.

<u>Procedure</u>:

At the conclusion of a seminar, workshop, or program, there is often a positive feeling among the participants regarding what they have learned. The task is to capture this enthusiasm and channel it toward the improvement of on-the-job performance.

As a closing device, distribute the form on the following page to all participants and ask them to complete it before they leave. They should then resolve to deliver it to their supervisors and engage them in discussion.

A closing quote may even be in order:

> "Upon the plains of hesitation bleach the bones of countless millions who, on the threshhold of victory, sat down to wait, and awaiting they died."

<u>Discussion Questions</u>:

1. What factors will serve to prevent you from implementing the desired changes? (e.g., non-supportive supervisor, time pressures, irrelevant material)
2. What steps can you take to ensure the likelihood of changing your behavior? (e.g., develop a support group or buddy system, solicit your supervisor's support, attend follow-up session)

<u>Materials Required</u>:

Form on the following page

<u>Approximate Time Required</u>:

5-15 minutes

<u>Source</u>:

The quote is anonymous, but initially provided by R. S. Juralewicz.

Letter to My Boss

Dear _____:

I have just completed a training program entitled "_____
_____." I want to tell you what I feel I
learned, and how I plan to change or improve as a result. I would
appreciate talking to you about the following ideas in the near
future. I will then solicit your active support in implementing
these changes.

Here is what I propose to do differently/better:

1.

2.

3.

4.

5.

6.

7.

8.

9.

10.

Signed_____

Date_____

Letter to Myself

Objective:

To facilitate transfer of training to the job.

Procedure:

At the conclusion of a training program or seminar, draw the participants' attention to the need for transfer of the new knowledge, skills, or attitudes obtained to the job, and the difficulty of doing so successfully. Then, briefly describe the merits of establishing a psychological contract for behavior change, and the requirements for a successful contract (see notes on the following page). Distribute the sample form and allow several minutes for its completion. Conclude the process by collecting the sealed envelopes and encouraging the participants to anticipate the receipt of a letter in 30 days.

Discussion Questions:

    1. What factors will serve to prevent you from implementing the desired changes? (e.g., non-supportive supervision; time pressures; irrelevant material)
    2. What steps can you take to increase the likelihood of changing your behavior? (e.g., develop a support group or buddy system; solicit your supervisor's support; attend follow-up sessions)

Materials Required:

Form on the following page

Approximate Time Required:

5-15 minutes

Source:

Unknown. A recent adaptation was presented as an "Individual Action Plan" by Scott Parry in "Why Training Programs Succeed and Fail," Training, August, 1979, pp. 9, 12.

Contracting with Yourself

Psychological Contract:

A commitment to yourself or others to make a change.

Requirements:

    1. Awareness of a problem (e.g., I smoke 30 cigarettes a day and that may lead to cancer).
    2. Desire to change (I would like to quit smoking).
    3. Statement of objective (Within 30 days, I will stop smoking):
        a. Clear
        b. Attainable
        c. Definite time frame
    4. Plan for review of progress (I will reduce my level of smoking by one cigarette per day. I will count the number smoked and post my progress on a big chart in front of my desk.)
    5. Meaningful reward (If I succeed, and sustain my abstinence for 6 months, I will treat myself to a vacation in _____.)

_____

Directions:

Write yourself a letter, committing yourself to a change in behavior as a product of this seminar. Sign it, insert it in the envelope, address it to yourself, and we will mail it back for your review in one month.

Dear _____:

_____

_____

_____

_____

_____

_____

_____

Sincerely,

_____